THE BIBLE AND THE QUR'AN

JACQUES JOMIER, O.P.

THE BIBLE AND
THE QUR'AN

Translated from the French
by
Edward P. Arbez

Foreword by Stephen K. Ray

IGNATIUS PRESS   SAN FRANCISCO

Original French edition: *Bible et Coran*
Les Éditions du Cerf © 1959

English translation: © 1964 by Desclée Company
(Some chapters rewritten by the author for the English edition)
Published with ecclesiastical approval
Reprinted by permission of Les Éditions du Cerf

Cover art: Raphael (1483–1520)
The Transfiguration
Scala/Art Resource, New York

Ascent of Muhammad to Heaven on Buraq,
Guided by Gabriel and Escorted by Angels
Ms. Or. 2265, fol. 195a. Safavid Dynasty.
British Library, London
Copyright Art Resource, New York

Cover design by Riz Boncan Marsella

Published in 2002 by Ignatius Press, San Francisco
All rights reserved
ISBN 0-89870-928-8
Library of Congress Control Number 2002105230
Printed in the United States of America ∞

CONTENTS

FOREWORD

In preparing this brief foreword to Ignatius Press' very welcome reprint of Jacques Jomier's impressive *The Bible and the Qur'an*, the title of another book, written a half-century ago, springs to mind: *Ideas Have Consequences,* by Richard M. Weaver of the University of Chicago. The title is a lesson in itself.

Two searing examples from the last century and a half amply demonstrate the truth of this assertion: the Communist Manifesto and *Mein Kampf.* Millions died, and more millions were ruined, because of the odious opinions set forth in these two documents. Streams of refugees, hopeless and broken, irrigated the no man's land of the twentieth century.

Ideas indeed have consequences. If, for example, a society is persuaded that cows are sacred, those beasts will wander about unhindered and be treated with an almost liturgical deference, even if large sections of the populace are often on the brink of starvation. This holds famously true in parts of India, whereas we in Europe and the Americas have a different perspective on cows, seeing them as producers of dairy products and meat.

Judaism, Christianity, and Islam each have their respective sacred books. And each has had and will continue to have far-reaching consequences. Frequently, they will be consequences in deadly conflict.

The Hebrew Scriptures are, of course, the Christian Old Testament. To these Hebrew Scriptures, Christianity added the New Testament. And Islam claims that its sacred book, the Qur'an, is the word of God. All three of these religions and their scriptures have important things in common, especially the doctrine that there is only one God. Yet this commonality is limited by insurmountable disagreements about God's nature, man, and salvation.

Some questions immediately present themselves: To whom has God revealed his truth? Is God one Person or three? Does God have a Son? Could God become man: the Incarnation? Or is the very idea blasphemous? Is he a Father of sons and daughters, as in the Judeo-Christian tradition, or a Master of slaves, as Islam maintains? These are not small matters, and the disagreements issuing from the differences are potentially explosive: cultures and nations historically have been at each other's throats. The Old Testament is the book of God's revelation to the people of Israel. It is a record of God's law; his covenants; his signs and wonders; and the religious life and history of his covenant people. It also contains the promise of a coming Messiah—the Anointed One—the one who will extend the covenant and salvation to all the nations. The Jews awaited this Messiah.

Finally, he came. He fulfilled the prophecies of the Jewish Scriptures, but his own people rejected him because they could not accept the idea that God could become flesh. No one had seen God, since he is a spirit. How could God become a man? Such a claim was ludicrous to the Jews. And even if God had taken on flesh, it was inconceivable that he would suffer such an ignominious death as crucifixion. But this is precisely what Jesus Christ did.

Most refused to believe; but many did, giving rise to historical Christianity. The bodily Resurrection of Jesus from the dead at a certain time and at a certain place guaranteed the truth of the Christian claim. God had taken on human nature so that men could become partakers of the divine nature. Catholic philosopher Frederick D. Wilhelmsen sums it up most eloquently in the opening sentences of his philosophical masterstroke *The Metaphysics of Love*:

> When God descended from heaven, man arose from the grave of antiquity and shook off the winding sheet of despair. He walked erect and spoke the name which is His being: Son of God in Christ His Brother

As in Judaism, in Islam the very idea of a God-Man is impossible. It is blasphemous. Indeed, Islam understands itself to be a return to basics, as it were: a linking back to the pristine monotheism of Abraham, shorn of all the impurities and accretions of Judaism and Christianity. It teaches that "the greatest of prophets" came from seventh-century Arabia. Muhammad is his name. He is The Prophet. Though God spoke through men such as Adam, Noah, Abraham, Moses, David, and Jesus, Muhammad is "the seal of the prophets", for through him came the perfect revelation, the Qur'an.

Muhammad supposedly accepted the revelation of God to the Israelites and in the Gospel of Jesus; but, the Qur'an contradicts the Bible in very important ways. And this raises very important questions. For instance, does the Bible give any grounds for thinking God intended to give a further revelation after the revelation of Jesus? Does it tell us that it will be superseded by a new revelation? Does it foretell another prophet, who would complete the New Testament?

Christians will of necessity argue that the answer to all of these questions is No. Islam's claim to the fullness of divine revelation cannot be correct, for God has already sent his Son, his final Word (Jn 1:1). There is no fuller revelation to come. There is no greater prophet than the Word made flesh. The writer of Hebrews puts it best: "In many and various ways God spoke of old to our fathers by the prophets; but in these last days he has spoken to us by a Son" (Heb 1:1). The *Catechism* adds, "Christ, the Son of God made man, is the Father's one, perfect, and unsurpassable Word. In him he has said everything; there will be no other word than this one" (CCC 65).

What more could God say? He revealed the mystery by giving us his very self. Jude tells us that we are to "contend for the faith which was once for all delivered to the saints" (Jude 3). Catholics believe that the revelation given "once for all" can be more deeply understood and that doctrine can develop as this understanding increases, but they (along with Protestants and Orthodox Christians) reject claims of other prophets having a fuller message from God than that of Jesus.

How do Muslims account for the differences between the Qur'an and the biblical books of previous divine revelation that they supposedly also accept? If there is discontinuity between the Bible and the Qur'an, they argue, then it must be that the Jews and Christians have manipulated and altered the truth that God revealed to them.

Perhaps the most glaring theological difference between the Qur'an and the Christian Scriptures is in how the respective books treat the doctrine of the Incarnation. The New Testament, based on the historical fact of the Virgin Birth of the Eternal Son of God, who died for our sins and rose again, proclaims salvation for men and their inclusion into the family of God through the work of the Incarnate Word, Jesus Christ: "In the beginning was the Word, and the Word was with God, and the Word was God.... And the Word became flesh and dwelt among us" (Jn 1:1, 14). The Qur'an, on the other hand, rejects the idea of God becoming man. Muslims affirm the Virgin Birth of Jesus but vehemently deny his divinity. God can have no son, in the Muslim scheme of things, because that would imply that God had a "consort", which is clearly impossible. The Christian view that God's omnipotence means, among other things, that he can have a son without a "consort" is not addressed.

The word "Islam" means "submission", and Muslims submit to the teaching of the Qur'an as the word of God. Muhammad and the Qur'an are simply not to be questioned. Since Islam considers the religion of the Jews and Christians to be greatly inferior, Muslims usually do not compare their beliefs with the Bible.

Does the Qur'an teach truth? For the Christian, the answer is "Yes, but . . ." The Qur'an contains truth alongside error. Christianity and Islam, though having important doctrines in common, hold different views of God's relation to man. In some important respects, these views are mutually exclusive. Thus, both religions cannot be right. On certain important points—such as the identity and significance of Jesus Christ—Christianity and Islam fundamentally disagree.

Jerusalem showcases, as no other city does, the clash of these religions. A walk through the streets of Old Jerusalem reveals how deeply these related yet different religions can affect everyday life. Profound contrasts are found at every turn: the chanted prayers and blast of the ram's horn as Jews celebrate and weep at the Western Wall; the sound of bells ringing from Christian churches; and the wailing call to prayer sung by the muezzin from the Muslim minarets five times a day. Even differences about such things as how their respective adherents dress, what they eat, the kind of schools they create, their family lives, and architecture are shaped by Judaism, Christianity, and Islam.

This war of ideas is made unmistakably manifest in the streets of the Holy City by the rumble of tanks and the sound of distant gunfire. The heart of Jerusalem is divided. It beats with the revealed truth of one God, yet it is torn by this conflict of theologies.

As Christians, we are to preach the gospel in season and out. To be better prepared to face the challenges presented by Islam, we must be at least acquainted with its tenets. Islam cannot be ignored. In numbers, it rivals Christianity, having over a billion adherents. It is a powerful force in the world, and all indications are that it will continue to gain ground. Christians must engage this religion, which can be both an ally and an intransigent enemy.

Jacques Jomier's analysis and insight will prove extremely helpful.

Stephen K. Ray
August 6, 2002
Jerusalem

TRANSLATOR'S PREFACE

Father Jomier's *The Bible and the Qur'an* is the work of a scholar well qualified by a long study of the matter and by his life in the Middle East. He never engages in controversy. He is satisfied with stating the facts from which the reader can draw his own conclusions. While the author remains objective throughout, his contact with the people of Islam has enabled him to maintain sympathy and charity toward them.

The author has kindly supplied a number of additions that have been embodied in the present text so that this translation may be regarded as a second edition.

In the original French text the quotations from the Qur'an are taken from the excellent French translation of Régis Blachère. For this edition it was thought preferable to go back to the original Arabic text of the Qur'an while taking into account the various English translations in difficult passages.

The translator wishes to thank his friend Mr. Grey Leslie for suggestions and advice at various points.

May we hope that this work of Father Jomier and others written in the same spirit may help to bring about a better understanding between Christians and Muslims and thus help the cause of the peace in the Middle East.

I

What Is the Qur'an?

The Qur'an is the sacred book of Islam. It comprises 114 chapters, or surahs, unequal in length. Altogether the book has 6,200 and some verses; therefore it is definitely shorter than the New Testament. It is written in Arabic, in a magnificent style that is still studied in the courses on Arabic literature as the first masterpiece of the language. The printing of its modern editions and the copying of the ancient manuscripts are faultless. Ignoring a material mistake would be regarded by Muslims as a very serious lack of respect for its sacred character.

The biblical revelation is spread over many centuries and has found expression in a multitude of books that differ considerably in character. The preaching of the Qur'an lasted only twenty years and was collected into a single volume.

Muhammad started preaching the Qur'an between A.D. 610 and 612. It all began in Mecca in the desert region of the Arabian peninsula. This large village had a water supply, but it had no cultivated land. Its territory was dry and stony. Its people made their living by the great caravan traffic. Their fairs and their places of worship drew merchants and pilgrims. The Hedjaz in which Mecca lies is halfway between Aden and the Mediterranean Sea; thus on one of the main ways followed by the caravans from India to Europe. Muhammad's activity up to that time did not differ from that of his fellow Meccans. He led traders' caravans and, as a

consequence of retreats and prayers, felt that he was especially favored with apparitions, dreams, or revelations of au-
ditory character. He had the impression of being in the
presence of a mysterious person who transmitted to him a
special message from God. At first he was dismayed, but his
relatives comforted him, and gradually some believers gathered around him in small groups; they lived according to his
directions, collected that Qur'anic preaching as a prophet's
disciple collects the sayings of his master; that is to say, as the
very Word of God. For twenty years, new revelations, which
were added to the initial sayings, kept coming. The opposition of unbelievers made the life of the primitive group of
believers difficult. Around 616 Muhammad sent some dozens of his followers to Ethiopia to escape mockery and vex-
ations. However, he himself remained in Mecca with his other
followers until 622. As the opposition grew more threatening, he led a general exodus to Medina, an oasis with cultivated lands some three hundred miles north of Mecca. There
the new community became a theocratic state under the authority of its leader, who then played the part of a prophet,
a lawgiver, and a warrior like Moses. When Muhammad died
in 632, after fighting for ten years by word and weapons, the
greater part of Central Arabia, including Mecca, had accepted Islam as the new religion.

During all that time the body of the Qur'anic revelations
delivered to the Muslims had been increasing constantly. Muhammad's death closed the era of these revelations; this is the
teaching of Islam. Muhammad was regarded as "the seal of
the prophets" (33, 40: *Khatama an nadiyina*), that is, the one
who definitively closed the series. Henceforth Muslims had
at their disposal what is called the Qur'an, "sacred text that
is recited", thus a collection of oracles, of narratives concerning biblical and other personages, and, finally, of teach-

ing both dogmatic and legislative or moral. As a whole, it showed God's action in the deeds of the new community, discussed the pagans, the Jews, and the Christians, and preached the divine unity and transcendence as well as the Last Judgment.

At first, the verses had been preserved in the memory of believers, who repeated them constantly in liturgical recitations and in prayerful vigils. However, some had been jotted down on makeshift material (ostraca, fragments of pottery, shoulder blades of camels, and so forth). Then, after 632, a collection was undertaken by private persons; this was the first written recension of the whole Qur'an, one or two years after Muhammad's death. Othman (the third Caliph, 644–655) was destined to take up again, twenty-five years later, the work on the Qur'an, and this resulted in an almost official version. A committee set up for that purpose gathered all the written documents; it questioned especially the very first believers and the close companions of the Prophet, for the oral tradition of the text had priority over the written tradition. The texts were grouped, though it was not possible to state accurately their chronological sequence. As a rule, the longest chapters are the most recent, but this is not true in all cases. The problem of the chronology of the different texts, therefore, is the first one that confronts, and will always confront, the exegesis of the Qur'an. However, it will be possible to distinguish, at least, the Meccan passages delivered for the first time in Mecca before 622 and the Medinan passages that belong to the last ten years of Muhammad (622–632). If it is impossible to date all the texts one would like, at least one can assign a certain number to their place in the history of the primitive community.

Arabic writing, a kind of shorthand, was still more defective then than it is today. In the seventh century of our era, there were no diacritical points to differentiate several consonants expressed primitively by one and the same sign (thus b, t, th, y); the short vowels, even at times the long vowels, were not expressed. Hence the possibility of confusions that only oral tradition could prevent. Later several improvements were adopted in the writing of Othman's Qur'an; the points and the vowels were used. Less than two centuries after the death of the Prophet, everything had been definitively fixed except some minor differences of reading, which were collected carefully. It should be noted that the first complete private recension of the Qur'an dates from one or two years after the death of Muhammad; thus some twenty years after the promulgation of the oldest texts. The official revision of that recension (that of the Caliph Othman) took place twenty years after the death of the Prophet, therefore, forty years after the beginning of Islam. Note that the collecting of the text of the Qur'an into one single corpus was made more quickly than the complete writing of our Gospels. But the twenty or forty years that passed before the quasi-official edition of Othman brings us close to the thirty or forty years between the beginning of the ministry of Jesus and the composition of the Synoptic Gospels.

In either case we are dealing with oral civilizations, and the fidelity of the memory of the believers of the first generation is of greater importance than the precise date of the writing.

For further information on these matters, the reader may refer to the bibliography at the end of this book.

2

Translations of the Qur'an

Muslim scholars insist on the beauty of the form of the Qur'an in its Arabic text, its wonderful style, the conciseness of its wording, the striking, incisive character of its language, its rhythm—all making a strong appeal to the hearts of the hearers.

To believers, such considerations are not merely matters of feelings or esthetics. Muhammad did not claim the power of working miracles, though believers, at times, challenged him to do so (17:92ff.). His miracle was the Qur'an itself, which he describes as something inimitable, a unique book that could only come from God.

The question of the uniqueness of the Qur'an is thus a dogmatic matter, and, therefore, we should not be surprised at the attitude of Muslim scholars on the question of translating the Qur'an. Most admit that it is possible to translate the "ideas" of the Qur'an in order to spread the knowledge of Islam. But such renderings should not be regarded as the Qur'an itself and should not be used in liturgical services.

In our references to the text of the Qur'an, the first numeral is that of the surah, or chapter; this is followed by a colon and the second number, which is that of the verse according to ordinary numbering adopted in most translations. A slanting line may follow. The numeral after the slanting line is that of the verse according to the Arabic version published in Cairo. Thus 2:21/23 means surah, or chapter, 2, verse 21 (common numbering) /23 (Cairo Arabic numbering).

Some theologians hold less rigid views and allow those who have no knowledge of Arabic to use the vernacular in texts from the Qur'an for ritual prayer. In Turkey, however, a Turkish translation of the Qur'an was substituted in place of the Arabic text, and this caused considerable commotion in the Islamic world.

The Qur'an has been translated into a great number of languages. A list of some of the most important scholarly translations into English will be found in the bibliography at the end of this book. A comparison of different good translations often will help in clarifying the text of the original, if not in removing all of the obscurities.

For a good survey of translations beginning with the Latin translation made at the instigation of Abbot Petrus Cluniacensis (1092–1156), the reader will find valuable information in Régis Blachère's *Introduction au Coran*, 2d ed. (Paris, 1977), pp. vii–xxxviii.

3

Muhammad's Universal Mission according to the Qur'an

In order to understand Islam, it is necessary in the first place to realize for whom the new religion was meant. It was born in a well-defined desert region of Arabia. Did it have, from the very beginning, the dynamism that was to make it formidable enough to reach the end of Asia and Africa? Was Muhammad, from the start, conscious of the part he was to play in the religious history of mankind? Or is it only gradually, as a consequence of the military successes of the Arab conquest that the Muslims discovered the strength of their movement?

At present, Muslim tradition holds a position that was quickly adopted in Islam. Generally, Muslims regard Muhammad as the last of the prophets; as the one sent by God to all mankind; as one whose mission is to last until the end of the world. Gradually Muslim tradition adopted the following view of the religious history of the world. According to its teachings, Islam is a religious attitude written by God in human nature. It was the religion of all the prophets and of all righteous men since creation. Its extremely simple dogma has never changed. It appears in identical form in the faith of

The text of this chapter was completely rewritten by the author for this translation.

Adam, Noah, and Abraham; it is the core of the message that Moses, Jesus, and Muhammad announced.

Only the legislations may have differed; some commandments that no longer suited new conditions were abrogated and replaced by others. As a Muslim commentator puts it, in the history of the world there is only one true religion, but there have been several different legislations.

Muslim tradition also regards Judaism and Christianity as true religions that were forms of the one true religion, valid for a special period of history. For Muslim tradition the missions of Moses and Jesus were limited in time and space. God sent Moses and Jesus only to the children of Israel; but Muhammad came with a mission to the whole world. The Qur'anic Islam is to take the place of all the older forms of the one religion that is engraved in man's nature. The Qur'an has done away with the prior legislations. The Jewish legislation and the Christian legislation are regarded as obsolete. Islam only allows Jews and Christians to obey their legislations within their respective communities until both groups embrace Islam and join the community of the last period of history; that is to say, the Islamic community. According to Muslim teaching, Jews and Christians will find in the Qur'an that which is essential and best in the Torah and the Gospel. Indeed, the doctrine of the Qur'an appeared under the sign of a certain syncretism. It mixed together many Jewish and Christian elements, to which it gave a new form.

In the main, this is the common position held by the tradition of Islam, as it lives in practice at the present time. However, it may be asked whether this agrees with the historical reality of the first age of Islam. What does the Qur'an tell us of Muhammad's mission? Was he sent only to the Arabs in whose midst he lived, whose language he spoke? Or does the Qur'an envisage a wider, universal mission? Orientalists have scrutinized the problem without agreeing on the answer. Both views are defended by scholars. Some hold that the Qur'an teaches a universal mission of Muhammad; others think that the Qur'an assigns only a mission to the Arabs. We wish to present briefly the different arguments before drawing our conclusion.

1. The Qur'an presents Muhammad's mission as of special interest to the Arabs in the first place. His task was to convert people who had never had prophets speaking their language. Thus God addresses Muhammad:

> You were not on the side of the mountain [Sinai] when We called [Moses]; but you came through a mercy from your Lord that you may warn a people to whom no warner came before you. (28:46)

This mission corresponds to the idea that God has sent a prophet to each community:

> And surely We have raised in each community a messenger (rasul), [saying]: Worship God [Allah]. (16:38/36)

The preaching of the Qur'an in Arabic, therefore, is addressed to the Arabs among whom Muhammad lived:

> And so We revealed to you an Arabic Qur'an that you may warn the Mother of the cities [the Mother of the city = Mecca] and those around it, and that you may warn regarding the day of gathering in which, there is no doubt, a party shall be given in the garden and a party in the flames. (42:5/7)

But is it right to pay attention to those texts only? An exegete who would dwell on some texts of the Old and New Testaments could as well restrict the action of the Old Testament prophets to the Jewish people by ignoring all the repercussions that the history of that people was to have in the history of universal salvation. Indeed in the Psalms and in the prophets there are passages that announce that the salvation of the world shall come through the people of the Old Testament. If one should take only the Qur'anic texts that limit Muhammad's mission, there is no reason for not understanding similarly the words of Christ describing His mission as concerned with the lost sheep of the house of Israel. A mission addressing itself primarily to a specially defined social group and through that group to a much wider collectivity is one thing, and a mission limited precisely to that social group is another thing.

2. The preaching activity of Muhammad and of the first Muslims exerted itself in the geographical and sociological framework of Mecca and surrounding regions. However, we should not forget the migration to a non-Arabian land, Abyssinia, of several dozens of Muslims and the relations that followed with the Abyssinian Christians.

3. Surely, according to the Qur'an itself, a number of the Muslim positions developed under the influence of circumstances. Some ideas appeared only gradually. In Mecca, the mission of Muhammad was defined as that of a prophet, a preacher who warned his people. Later, in Medina, his mission was that of a military and political leader. Therefore, it cannot be affirmed that in the Qur'an such a position is final so long as it has not been tested by experience; and in order that it may stand such a test, there must be favorable circumstances. For instance, in Mecca where the Muslims were too weak to take up arms, there could be no question of hegemony by force. They had to bide their time until circumstances changed, until a choice was possible between clemency and force in a concrete case, in order to know what the final decision would be.

4. The fact that Muhammad preached only to the Arabs of Mecca and the surrounding regions does not constitute a

proof that according to the Qur'an his mission was limited
to the Arabs. This would be a mathematical reasoning out of
place in this case. In Mecca everything was still too vague,
too doubtful for the problem to be posed concretely and,
therefore, for a valid solution to be given. Thus, for instance,
in Mecca, between the years 610 and 622, we notice a global
sympathy of the Muslims for those who received the Scripture before them. But that sympathy is something hazy, with
an indefinite halo. Does it mean that Muhammad admits all
that which the people of the Scripture hold and therefore he
will not intervene in their affairs when the occasion presents
itself? It would be rash to affirm this, in spite of the vague-
ness of the Qur'an in its statements about the older "sacred
books", the name of which is not mentioned in Mecca (except in a text that is perhaps later). One sees, however, two
points that will not fail to modify the situation, when the
Muslims will have to face them squarely. On the one hand,
the old surahs are aware of the divisions among the people of
the Scripture; on the other hand, they very soon take a stand
against the idea that Jesus was more than a privileged creature of God.

Let us examine these two points. First, the existence of sects
and parties is affirmed. The people of Mecca had traveled and
had met with adherents of the various sects. They had seen
monks, known slaves and freedmen of Mecca. Even though
they did not enter into the particulars of the theological controversies, it was easy to notice the divisions. In the second place,
the Qur'an takes even then a stand against the idea of the divinity of Christ. This question concerned a perfectly intelligible attitude. The pagans of Mecca knew that the divinity of
Christ was disputed. One did not have to be a theologian to
understand that some saw in Jesus more than a privileged creature of God, while others regarded Him as a man.

The following verses, taken from a surah dating from the middle of the Meccan period, will show how aware they were of those divisions and of the questions about the person of Jesus. The people concerned here are the pagans of Mecca, and the text is addressed to Muhammad:

> And when the son of Mary is propounded as an example, your people turn away from him [or raise a clamor at it]. (43:57/58)

Immediately after this, the Qur'an goes on with a declaration that:

> Jesus was only servant to whom We granted favors, and We made him an example for the Children of Israel. (43:59)

A few verses farther on it refers to the divisions among the Children of Israel:

> The parties (*ahzab*) differed among themselves then; therefore, woe to those who are unjust because of the torment of a painful day. (43:65)

Such a situation forebodes the day when, in Medina, Muhammad will intervene in the affairs of the Jews and Christians and will declare outright that he regards himself as sent to them, as destined to bring light on the substance of their divisions; therefore, as having a message to transmit to them:

> O People of the Scripture, Our messenger has come to you, clarifying after an interruption [of the mission] of the messengers, lest you say: There has not come to us anyone bringing the good news or any warner. So there has come to you one bringing the good news, a warner, and God is almighty. (5:19/22)

5. It is, therefore, impossible to specify the extent of the mission that the Qur'an recognizes as Muhammad's while

the ambiguities subsist. Gradually one sees that the mission attributed to Muhammad is not limited by geographical or ethnological boundaries. There is the question of a message that is to be delivered and of an increasingly clearer consciousness that nothing can resist a prophet.

The problem, first of all, is to ensure the victory of the oneness of God over paganism; to correct the errors of the Jews and Christians, particularly about the person of Jesus; finally, to further the spread of the Muslim community.

Such are the aims that Muslims will ever keep before them and that will guide the noblest minds among them, even if the attraction of glory and booty plays a great part in the movement to spread Islam.

Does the Qur'an envisage a conquest of the world? Not explicitly, it would seem. But a community that, by its internal dynamism, looked to the fulfillment of that threefold ideal, was bound to move forward beyond the borders of Arabia and carry on in the whole world what it had begun in the deserts of the Hedjaz.

If the Muslims had found in Arabia or outside Arabia the theoretical forms of Judaism and Christianity that they imagined to be the true forms, possibly they would have stopped. But that theoretical Judaism and Christianity existed only in their imagination, or perhaps in certain aberrant sects scattered through the Near East. Conscious as they were of being the Knights of the divine Oneness, and the reformers of Judaism and Christianity, they allowed themselves to be carried farther; and so, according to our view, Muslim tradition is in perfect logical agreement with the facts when it affirms Muhammad's universal mission. The Qur'an teaches, at least implicitly, this universality to the extent that it exalts the person of Muhammad who goes forward and will not brook the least contradiction.

Moreover, no text of the Qur'an limits the impetus of that internal dynamism.

6. In the Qur'an itself Muslims noted a certain number of verses as justifying their position. The significance of those verses has been discussed by some Orientalists, as for instance Fr. Buhl. This specialist has tried to restrict the force of the terms "world" or "men" by showing that sometimes the Qur'an uses them in a restricted sense. If one does not take into account the psychological context, such exegesis could be defended. Nevertheless, those texts express a deep feeling that Muhammad has an immensely important part to play. This is a considerable element in the formation of that internal dynamism that will sweep away all obstacles. In several texts that date from the middle of the Meccan period, Muhammad's mission is described as a mercy to the world, as a mercy for the world:

We have not sent you but as a mercy to all nations. (21:107)

And again:

Blessed is He who sent down the *Furqan*[1] upon his servant that he may be a warner to the worlds [the peoples of the world]. (25:1)

Or again:

And We have not sent you but universally to [all] men as a bringer of good news and as a warner, but most men do not know. (34:27/28)

Also:

Say, O men, I am the messenger (*rasul*) of God to you all, of Him to whom belongs the kingdom of the heavens and the

[1] This word *Furqan* is understood as discrimination between true and false, or salvation, deliverance, and so on.

earth. There is no God but He. He gives life and causes death.
So, believe in God and His messenger (*rasul*), the *Ummi*[2]
prophet who believes in God and His words, and follow him
that you may be guided aright. (7:157/158)

Moreover, the Qur'an itself is addressed to the pagans of
Arabia as well as to the Jews and Christians. From the beginning of the Medinan period on, the latter are commanded to believe in Muhammad's mission, therefore in the
authenticity of the Qur'an. This confirms what we said earlier about Muhammad's claim to prophetic authority over
Jews and Christians. The history of the beginnings of Islam
shows that the Christians and the few Jews who believed in
Muhammad's mission during his lifetime immediately became a part of the new community. The toleration that Jews
and Christians enjoyed (when they were not converted but
refrained from fighting Islam) is no justification of their condition, from the Muslim point of view. It is a concession to
their hardness of heart from a purely social point of view.
The Qur'an is clear:

> He who refuses to believe in all the prophets, therefore in
> Muhammad, cannot enter paradise.

Therefore Islam considers the history of the world as dom-
inated by only one religion. God sent the prophets to the
different people to teach it to men. The dogma has not
changed, but the legislation was modified. For the Muslims,

---

[2] The meaning of *Ummi* is disputed: gentile, unlettered, and so on. On the
question of whether Muhammad was unlettered, whether he could read or
write, see Richard Bell, *Introduction to the Qur'an* (Edinburgh: University Press,
1953), pp. 17ff. Bell remarks, "It has become almost a dogma with Muslims
that the Prophet was unable to read or write. It enhances the miracle of the
Qur'an that it could have been delivered by one entirely unlettered."

all the prophets sent before Muhammad had missions limited in time and space. Muhammad alone was given a universal message. According to them, the Islam of the Qur'an is destined to be the religion of all men until the end of the world. A statement of the Qur'an teaches that Muhammad is the last of the prophets:

> Muhammad is not the father of any of your men, but he is the messenger of God and the seal of the prophets. (33:40)

Henceforth, according to the Muslim view of history, no new prophet is to be expected until the Last Judgment. Though Muslims expect the return of Jesus before the end of the world, they do not look for any religious change from His coming. He will play only a subordinate part in the service of Islam.

The rhythm of the periods into which the history of the world before Muhammad was divided by the alternating missions of prophets and the periods of indifference is now broken:

> This day the unbelievers have despaired [of turning you away] from your religion; so do not fear them but fear me! Today I have perfected for you your religion and I have completed my favor on you and accepted Islam as a religion. (5:5/3)

4

The Qur'an Appeals to the Bible

For Islam, then, the history of the world is divided into periods in which prophets are the dominant figures. Islam believes in all those prophets; it believes in the Scriptures brought by those prophets. It believes in the Torah (*Tawrat*), the Scripture given by Moses to the Children of Israel. It believes in the Gospel (*Injil*) given by Jesus to the Children of Israel also. But, above all, it believes in the Qur'an, which is *the* Scripture of Islam preeminently, the sacred book of the last period of history. These three books are regarded by Muslims as the Word of God. Each of them confirms the truth of its predecessors. Thus, for instance:

> And certainly We [God] sent Noah and Abraham, and We put in their offspring the gift of prophecy and Scripture (*al-Kitab:* the Book). So among them there are some who are guided aright, but many of them act wickedly.
> Then We caused our messengers to follow in their footsteps, and We made Jesus, son of Maryam, to follow, and We gave him the *Injil* [Gospel], and We put, in the hearts of them that followed him, compassion and mercy. (57:26/27)

As for the Qur'an, from the Muslim standpoint, it itself confirms the earlier Scriptures. Thus the following words addressed by God to Muhammad:

> This is a blessed Scripture (*Kitab*) that We have brought down [revealed], verifying what was before it [the earlier Scriptures],

that you may warn the mother of cities [Mecca] and those
around it and those who believe in the next life. (6:92)

Indeed, the Qur'an takes up again many themes, ideas,
and narratives contained in the Bible. We will recall the most
important ones. The comparison of the themes, thoughts,
and narratives is not enough. With the same pieces of col-
ored stone, one can make different mosaics. We must thus
work out clearly the meaning that those biblical and Qur'anic
texts take when they are put back into their respective con-
texts. We shall try to do this at the end of the book.

5

The Qur'an Speaks of the Bible in High Terms, but Muslims Do Not Read the Bible

The Qur'an speaks very highly of the earlier Scriptures that were transmitted by the messengers of God. It is a duty for the Muslim to believe in those Scriptures and in those messengers of God:

> O believers, believe in God and His messenger and in the Scriptures that He brought down [revealed] to His messenger; and in the Scriptures that He revealed before. He who disbelieves in God and His angels and His Scriptures and His messengers and the Last Day, indeed he is in great error. (4:135/136)

The principle is quite clear, but the fulfillment of the duty is much more difficult. In practice, in what does the obligation consist? What is, in fact, the status of the Torah, the Psalms, the Gospel? At first the position of the Qur'an toward the older Scriptures was rather general. It began to become more definite only when Muhammad came into contact with the Jews of Medina.

In Mecca, excepting some very rare cases that may belong to a later period—Medinan texts that found their way into Meccan sections—the Qur'an does not try to distinguish between Jews and Christians. It does not use those words, though

it refers to Moses and Jesus; but it speaks of the "Children of
Israel". There is, then, no question as yet of Torah or *Injil*,
but only of the Scripture or Book (*Kitab*). So in the text of
the surah of Maryam. When Mary brings her child, the people are scandalized because she is not married. But the child
in the cradle vindicates Mary:

> Mary brought [the child] to her people. They said: Mary,
> surely you have done a strange thing. Mary pointed to [the
> child]. They said: How should we speak to a child in the
> cradle? He said: I am a servant of God. He gave me the Scrip-
> ture (*al-Kitab*) and made me a prophet (*nabi*); and He blessed
> me [literally: made me blessed], wherever I may be, and He
> enjoined on me prayer (*salat*) and almsgiving (*sakat*) while I
> live, and kindness to my mother, and He did not make me
> proud, unhappy. And peace on me on the day I was born
> and on the day I will die and on the day I will be raised alive
> from the dead. (19:28–34/27–33)

Likewise Moses received the Scripture:

> And certainly We gave Moses (*Musa*) the Scripture (*al-
> Kitab*) that they might be guided aright. (23:51/49)

The Qur'an speaks further (87:18/19) of the first pages
(leaves) of Abraham and Moses.

During the years of his preaching in Mecca the Prophet
saw Islam within the perspective of the earlier biblical religions. The faithful who believed in the biblical revelation
formed then only one community. After speaking of a long
line of prophets of the past, in the surah of the prophets, the
Qur'an adds:

> Verily this community of yours is only one community, and
> I am your Lord, therefore worship Me. And they became

divided among themselves. To Us all must come back. (21:92–93)

The Prophet does not dwell on the divisions among the people of the Scripture. This he will do a little later. Those divisions are known; even in the Meccan period the Qur'an often mentions the parties among the Children of Israel, but it calls the people especially to unity and dwells on the unity of God's messengers. The Prophet is with them against the pagans of Mecca. At that time there is no question of a possible contradiction between the Qur'an and the religious texts then in the hands of the people of the Scripture. The Qur'anic preaching recalls many narratives about the holy characters of the Old and New Testaments.

The Qur'an even definitely urges Muhammad, if he should have some doubt, to obtain a confirmation by consulting people who have read the earlier Scriptures:

> But if you are in doubt regarding what We have revealed to you, ask them who read the Scripture (al-Kitab) [revealed] before you. (10:94)

On the other hand, in Medina, though the Prophet speaks of the Children of Israel whom God has preferred over the rest of the world and though he still presents Jesus as sent to the Children of Israel, the Qur'an expresses itself more precisely. Then there is mention made of the Torah, *Injil* (Gospel), of Jews and Christians (*Nasara*). But what do these terms really mean? We are accustomed to take them in the sense given them in the Mediterranean countries, but Muslims understood them in the sense given them by the commentators of the Qur'an. In fact, what is the sense of Torah, or of *Injil* (Gospel)? This is not always clear. It would be an error to see in them the complete Old and New Testaments. There were several Gospels. The Jews were known in Medina, but who were the *Nasara*? There were many Christians and Christian sects, probably also Judeo-Christian sects. Therefore, it would be rash to reason as if only Orthodox Melkites, Jacobites, and Nestorians were meant. There is great uncertainty concerning the kind of Christians known to Muhammad. The history of monotheism in the heart of Arabia before Islam is extremely obscure for lack of evidence. We know a little about the Christian Arab tribes along the borders of Byzantium and Persia; but between Damascus and Mecca, there are more than some thousand miles, which we must take into account.

In Medina, the Jews were a large part of the population (three tribes out of five). The Qur'an soon called upon them to believe in Muhammad, therefore to follow him, for a prophet is entitled to obedience by those to whom he is sent. The Qur'an asked the Jews to pray with those who bow down. At that time Jews and Muslims prayed in the same direction (*kibla*), turned toward Jerusalem:

> Children of Israel, remember My favor that I bestowed on you and fulfill the covenant with Me, [as] I fulfill the covenant with you ... and believe in what I have sent down [revealed to Muhammad]; it confirms [the revelation] that you have [already]; be not the first to disbelieve, and do not barter My revelations for a mean price. Fear me and do not obscure truth with falsehood, nor conceal the truth knowingly. Perform the prayer (*salat*) and give the poor-tax (*sakat*) and bow down [in worship] with those who bow down. (2:38–40/41–43)

Some months later, as the Medinan Jews refused to follow Muhammad, the Qur'an gave the order to change the *kibla*. Henceforth the Muslims turned to the Ka'ba (the square temple) at Mecca in prayer. The direction of the prayer was for Muhammad an external sign that made it possible to tell his followers from other people.

In the controversy in Mecca between Muslims and Jews, the question of the Sacred Scriptures played a considerable part. The Muslims continued to proclaim their faith in the earlier messengers of God and in the revealed Books (Torah, Psalms, *Injil*). This article of their creed is quite firm. Even today, Muslims believe in the mission of Moses and Jesus and in the Books brought by them. But what does this faith mean in practice? They suspect the correctness of the present state of those Books and therefore limit themselves to the Qur'an. They do not read our Scriptures.

That remark may appear exaggerated to some Muslims, especially to certain missionary Muslims in Europe who occasionally open the Bible and the Gospels. Still, these men represent a very small minority. And whereas the Christian people, through liturgical texts and readings, are constantly in contact with the Old Testament, without mentioning those who read it directly, the Muslim people never use biblical texts or the Gospels in their official prayers. They know the Bible only through the Qur'an.

6

Does the Qur'an Teach That the Books of the Bible Have Been Tampered With?

Indeed the Qur'an accuses the Jews of misusing their Sacred Books, but it is difficult to see the precise point of the accusation. Although the question has been examined frequently, the results of the studies are still uncertain.

Sometimes definite persons seem to be meant. The Qur'an condemns some Jews for not following the Torah, which is in their possession. In this case, the Qur'an apparently supposes that they have a correct text of the Scripture. Otherwise there would be no point in the accusation:

> Do you enjoin what is just and proper (*birr*) upon men and forget [it] yourselves though you read the Book [Scripture]? Do you then not understand? (2:41/44)

Elsewhere the Qur'an makes accusations of tampering with the text, of a lack of loyalty on the part of the Jewish opponents who are supposed to have willfully concealed part of what they knew. The Qur'an even suggests the possibility of forgeries.

> Woe to them who write the Book [Scripture] (*al-Kitab*) with their hands, then say: This is from God, in order that they may make a small profit by it. And woe to them for what their hands have written, and woe unto them for their profit. (2:73/79)

Does the Qur'an here have in view some individual groups? Or the whole group of Jews?

Elsewhere the accusation is general, but then there is no question of writing false texts. Apparently the reference is to distorting the sense and forgetting part of the revelation, but the precise point of the accusation remains obscure. Thus:

> For breaking their covenant, We have cursed them and We have hardened their hearts. They distort the sense, and they forget a part of that of which they were admonished. You will continue to discover treachery from them, except a few of them. But forgive and pardon them. Behold God loves those who act kindly. (5:16/13)

What may be said at least is that the question remains obscure. There are people who forge texts and pass them off as revealed. All of the Jews are placed under suspicion, but at the same time the Qur'an tells them that they should follow Muhammad, because the ancient Scriptures in their possession foretell his coming. It is hard to see clearly in the heat of polemics. Yet, the Qur'an is very clear when it affirms that the older Scriptures had announced the coming of the Prophet:

> Write for us a fine reward in this world and in the next. Lo! We have become Jews to you. He said . . . I shall write it for those who are God-fearing and give the *sakat* [poor-tax], and those who believe in Our signs, those who follow the messenger (*rasul*), the *Ummi* prophet whom they will find written about with them in the *Towrat*, and the *Injil*. He will enjoin upon them what is good and forbid them what is wrong. (7:155–56/156–57)

Again:

> When Jesus, son of Mary, said: Children of Israel, behold I am the messenger (*rasul*) of God to you, confirming what

was revealed before Me in the *Towrat* [Torah] and bringing the good news of a messenger (*rasul*) who will come after Me, whose name shall be *Ahmad*. (61:6)

The situation supposed in the text just quoted must be understood from the psychological point of view. Muhammad was calling upon the "people of the Book" to believe in him and to follow him. They did not obey his call; they argued that their Scriptures did not announce the coming of the Arabian Prophet. The Medinan Jews, some of whom practiced usury and did not particularly relish the Arabian Prophet, especially not the theocratic rule of the Muslims, soon became the objects of personal attacks. This meant fighting. In the struggle the Muslims firmly upheld the principle of their faith in the prophets of the earlier Scriptures. But in practice they impugned the good faith and honesty of the Jews who had the Torah in their possession. It was but a step to questioning their interpretation of the text of the Torah; and soon the Muslims could proceed to questioning the correctness of the text of the Torah and suspecting forgeries. Some texts of the Qur'an suggest that this was done when dealing with some Jews or some groups. But does the Qur'an actually say that the Jews as a body were concerned in this matter? It may be hard to say so definitely. Why then would the Qur'an blame some Jews for not living in conformity to the text they read if that text was not regarded as correct?

What happened at a later date? The medieval polemicists, excepting a few like Fakhr al-Dîn-Râzi (1149) or Îbn Khaldun (1332–1406), admitted that the text itself of the earlier Scriptures had been tampered with. They went beyond what the Qur'an says. Could they do otherwise? For a Muslim the Qur'an is the sole criterion of truth. As there were in the Sacred Books of Judaism and Christianity ideas that did not agree with Islam, they concluded that the passages in which these ideas were exposed were perverted. The idea of a perfect agreement between Torah, Gospel, and Qur'an could be defended only by supposing an ideal Torah and Gospel different from the texts actually in the hands of the Jews and Christians. The only other way to get out of the difficulty would be to interpret the Bible in a strictly Qur'anic way, as some Muslim theologians did.

Hence, in practice, Muslims, with very few exceptions, do not read our Scriptures. They look upon the Qur'an as containing all the truth, even on the true Judaism and true Christianity. It is enough for them. Their respect for the Torah and the Gospel is something abstract. Moreover, such an attitude is nothing new. The charge of a falsification had been in the air for some time. Numerous Gnostic or Syncretist sects of more or less Christian character had had recourse to the accusation. Their purpose was to justify their rejection of books or parts of books that did not agree with their teaching; each made its own selection, thus, for instance, the Marcionists, the heterodox Judeo-Christians, the Manicheans, and so forth.

7

The Qur'an Proclaims, Above All, the Greatness of God, One, Creator, Lord of the Universe, Almighty and Good

On this point, the Qur'an, the Old Testament, and therefore also the New Testament as continuing the Old Testament, follow the same spiritual line: that of absolute monotheism. Everything is seen as depending on God. He is the One who has created everything. To Him everything belongs. He is all-knowing. He is omnipotent. A religious poetic breath raises the thought to the Creator from the most varied forms of creatures.

The believer is called upon to marvel at the beauty of nature. The believer is reminded of what is about him, and the commonplace realities of daily experience are transfigured in a sublime perspective. There is abundant evidence revealing God's action in the beings one meets with in the desert, in the oases, or on the sea, by trading or fishing vessels.

In the Qur'an, as in Genesis, creation is a six-day work, but the Qur'an refers to these six days of creation only as a whole; it does not distribute the different works according to the several days:

Verily, your Lord is Allah [God], who created the heavens and the earth in six days; then He ascended to the throne.

> He covers the night with the day that follows it up quickly.
> [He made] the sun and the moon and the stars, held [liter-
> ally, bewitched] by His command. Is not creation His, and
> the command? Blessed be Allah, the Lord of the worlds! (7:54)

Notice the figure of the throne, which appears also in the
Bible, but still more frequently in the later rabbinic and apocalyptic literature.

> Allah is He who created seven heavens and as many earths,
> and the command comes down gently between them that
> you may know that Allah is omnipotent and that Allah en-
> compasses all things in knowledge. (65:12)

The seven heavens are not mentioned in Genesis. Notice
also the stylistic device that draws a lesson from the enumeration of the facts, recalls man to a religious attitude, or simply formulates a doxology or mentions one of the divine
attributes. The following text points out a thought we find
expressed repeatedly in the Qur'an. All creation praises God,
and man must join in those praises. (Compare the Psalms, or
the song of the three youths in the furnace, Daniel 3:51–90.)

> The seven heavens and the earth, and all that is therein, there
> is nothing that does not sing His praise. Verily, He is kind
> and forgiving. (17:46/44)

> Praise be to Allah, who has created the heavens and the earth
> and has appointed darkness and light. But those who disbe-
> lieve hold as equal with their Lord [other deities]. He it is
> who has created you from clay. He has set a term for you, a
> term determined with Him, still you dispute [doubt]. He is
> in the heavens and on the earth. He knows what you earn.
> (6:1–3)

This last text alludes to a thought expressed frequently in
the Qur'an: The unity of the cosmos is an argument for the

unity of God. There is only one creation without fault; therefore, only one Creator. The other deities that men put on an equal plane with God are not able to give being to the smallest of creatures.

A long list of creatures occurs in the beginning of surah 16; we might compare it with Psalm 104/103. It alludes in passing to another duty of man to which the Qur'an reverts ceaselessly. Man must thank God for all the favors he has received from Him. Thanksgiving is a deeply Muslim attitude toward God, as it is with Jews and Christians:

For you He has created the cattle; in them [from them] you have warm clothing and useful things, from them you [have flesh] to eat; and you have in them beauty when you drive home [flocks] in the evening, and when you lead out to pasture in the morning. They carry your loads to a land you could reach only with trouble to yourselves. Verily, your Lord is compassionate and merciful. (16:5–7)

Many other items are mentioned in this context—rain, water, mules, asses—favors that God grants to men.

Thus again:

He it is who has subjected the sea that you may eat fresh meat [fish] from it, and bring out from it ornaments that you wear and you [man] see ships plowing it. [This is] from his bounty, and perhaps you will give thanks. (16:14)

The greatness of God is recalled at the beginning of each surah (excepting the ninth surah) by a formula that in Islam takes the place of the Christian "In the name of the Father. . . ." It reminds one that every important action is done in the name of God the Merciful, the Compassionate, the so-called *Basmala*.

It is likewise evoked in the first surah, a text which a Muslim repeats so often, notably in his ritual prayer, and which takes the place of the Christian Our Father:

> In the name of God, Compassionate and Merciful.
> Praise to Allah, Lord of the worlds,
> Compassionate and Merciful,
> Master of the Day of Judgment.
> Thee we worship; Thee we beseech for help.
> Guide us on the right path,
> The path of those Thou hast favored, not of those against
>   whom Thou art angry, not of those who go astray.

It is mentioned in contrast when the Qur'an dwells on the insignificance of man born of a drop of human seed and formed in his mother's womb, in a manner that recalls Job 10:8–12:

> Verily We created man from an extract of clay; then We placed him as a drop of sperm in a secure place; then We made the drop a lump of clotted blood; then We made the lump a morsel of flesh; then We created [in] the morsel of flesh, bones, and We clothed the bones with flesh; then We made him [as] another creation. So blessed be Allah the best of creators! Then, behold, after that, surely you will die. Then, behold on the day of resurrection, you will be raised. . . . We are [never] unmindful of creation. (23:12–15)

Hence the believer's first duty is submission to God, a thought so characteristic of the new religion that it became known as Islam (surrender, submission to God) and the believer as one who submits (Moslem, Muslim):

> Your God is One God. So to Him submit and give good news to those who humble themselves, to those whose hearts tremble when Allah is mentioned and to those who are pa-

tient in whatever befalls them and perform the prayer (*salat*) and spend of what We have given them. (12:35–36/34–35)

Verily, the religion with Allah is Islam, and if [unbelievers] dispute with you, say: I have submitted myself to Allah, and [so do] those who follow me. (3:18/19)

This idea of submission to the will of God is expressed also in the Epistle of James 4:7. It may be noted in passing that this epistle is the New Testament writing that has most points of contact with Islam.

The future belongs to God. When making his plans, the Muslim will always respect God's right.

Do not say of anything: Surely I will do it tomorrow— except, if God wills. If you forget, remember your Lord and say: Perhaps my Lord will guide me to something nearer to the right course. (18:23/24)

See James 4:13–15: "Come now, you who say, 'Today or tomorrow we will go into such and such a town and spend a year there and trade and get gain'; whereas you do not know about tomorrow. . . . Instead you ought to say, 'If the Lord wills, we shall live and we shall do this or that.' "

Finally this complete expression will bring confidence and peace:

Those who believe and whose hearts rest in the remembrance of Allah, those who believe and do right, blessedness shall be theirs and a good place to return to. (13:28)

8

The Apocalyptic Elements: The "Day" and the Resurrection

The foregoing thoughts on the greatness of God are at the basis of all the monotheistic religions. In theory, the human spirit can find them through its own power. In fact, however, this is rather difficult.

But Judaism, Christianity, and Islam profess a certain number of other ideas that are beyond the limits of human reasoning and are matters of faith. First of all, these religions believe that God spoke through prophets, and among the prophets venerated by the three religions, many are the same. The great difference is that Judaism and Christianity are divided on the person of Jesus, though admitting the texts of the ancient prophets. They share the Old Testament in common. Islam, on the contrary, admits theoretically the same prophets as Judaism and Christianity, but it does not always ascribe the same messages to them. They all agree on the fact that God spoke, but each religion holds different positions on what He said.

Islam likewise admits the dogma of the resurrection of the body and retribution according to works and to the observance of a revealed law. It should be noted that we remain at the level of an essentially natural religion, for Islam definitely rejects everything supernatural, any participation through grace in God's own life (we must, however, distinguish the case of the mystics, who, over and above the explicit teaching of the Qur'an and the barriers set up by the "lawyers", strove after the intimacy of a life lost in God). But, in general, according to the known scholastic distinction, Islam accepts only the supernatural *quoad modum*, that is to say, a direct intervention of God in the history of the world to teach on several occasions the principles of natural religion, to reveal some of its unknown data freely determined by Him, to work miracles, and so forth. The resurrection of the body and the Last Judgment appear, in that fundamentally natural perspective, joined to a supernatural *quoad modum*; the eternal bliss promised to the elect will be purely natural. It is announced as an earthly paradise with natural enjoyments and higher, more subtle joys of knowledge, but still purely human. However, let us not forget that though the great mass of Muslims, even of *Ulemas* (Muslim religious leaders), have understood and still understand literally the description of paradise, some souls saw or see in it only a symbolic picture of a higher, ineffable happiness.

The framework of the description of the end of the world is that of the apocalyptic literature that flourished in Palestine, beginning with the book of Daniel. Most of the items of the description are to be found in noncanonical works. As it is impossible to reproduce all of them, it will suffice to give examples of those texts to suggest their character:

> When one [single] blow of the trumpet shall be sounded, and the earth and the mountains are moved away and pounded into dust with one smashing blow, on that day *the* event [shall] come to pass and the heavens shall be split open; on that day [heaven] will be rent. And the angels will be on the sides and eight [of them] will carry the throne of your Lord above them; on that day you will be exposed and no secret of yours will be hidden. (69:13–32)

Each receives his record and learns his fate. The text continues with an enumeration of the sins for which one is condemned.

In another passage there is the description of the Judgment:

> The whole earth shall be a handful to Him on the day of the resurrection, and the heavens are rolled up in His right hand. He is glorified and exalted above what they associate with Him. The trumpet is sounded and they swoon, all who are in the heavens and on the earth, except those whom God wills. Then the trumpet is sounded a second time, and behold they are standing waiting! And the earth shines with the light of her Lord, and the Book is set up and the prophets and the witnesses are brought in, and the Judgment takes place . . . with truth, without anyone being wronged. Each soul is requited for what it did. God knows perfectly what they do. Those who disbelieved are driven to *Jahannam* [hell] in groups, and the gates [of hell] are opened and its guards say to them: Did not messengers from among you come to you reciting the revelations of your Lord and warning you of the meeting of this your Day? They will say: Indeed! And the sentence of punishment for disbelievers [will] be passed [fulfilled]. It will be said [to them]: Enter the gates of hell to be there forever. How bad is the abode of the proud! (39:67–74)

In this account of the Judgment it will be noted that God's presence is referred to in veiled language; it is manifested by the light that illumines the earth. According to Blachère, the surah to which this text belongs represents a later stage of the Qur'anic preaching, contrary to the view of the Arabic edition published in Cairo.

The Judgment of the elect is described in terms parallel to those used in the case of the wicked:

> Those who will have been faithful to their Lord will be driven in groups to *al-Janna* [the Garden—paradise]. When they reach

it, the gates will be opened, the keepers will say to them: Peace upon you! (*Salam'aleykum*), you are good [or you will be happy]. So enter it to live forever; and [the elect] shall say: Praise to Allah, whose promise is fulfilled for us, and [who] has made us inherit the earth. We will occupy [what part] of the Garden (*Janna*) we will. How pleasant is the reward [wages] of those who do good! You [Muhammad] will see the angels pressing around the Throne, glorifying with the praise of their Lord. Between them it will be judged according to truth, and it will be said: Praise to Allah, Lord of the Worlds. (39:73/74)

We will not quote the texts about the *houris*, those maidens of paradise, mentioned in few places. The word means that the white of their eyes is intensely white and the black of their eyes intensely black. For a brief description of these beings of perfect beauty allotted to the elect, the companions of the Right, see 56:33–36. Those texts have been used and misused by controversialists and apologists beyond reason. It suffices to know that they give to the Muslim paradise a very different aspect from that of the Christian concept. For analogies we should rather look to the millenarian literature that advocates a millennium of earthly happiness.

The description of the torments of hell are also very vivid and picturesque. We find there the fire. Together with the fire, there are also most of the punishments known in apocalyptic literature.

The Qur'an also dwells on the fact that everything will be exposed on the day of Judgment; this idea appears even in the oldest surahs.

When the heavens shall be cleft asunder, when the stars shall be scattered, when the seas shall rush forth, when the graves shall be turned upside down, a soul shall know what it has sent before. (82:1–5)

The final blessedness is often described in terms of tangible things: precious clothing, splendid foods and fruit, with handsome youths waiting on the elect, and so forth.

The following verse, however, suggests a happiness of a spiritual nature:

> Thou, O soul that art at rest, return to thy Lord, satisfied, accepted. Enter My Garden among My servants. (89:27–30)

There is also an isolated text whose real meaning is disputed among commentators. Many have taken it as referring to a vision of God at the resurrection; others take the verse as meaning an expectation of God without a real vision:

> Faces on that day [shall be] resplendent, looking toward their Lord. (75:22/23)

These apocalyptic views, however, have nothing messianic about them. God alone is the Judge and King on that dread day.

9

Retribution according to Works and Salvation by Faith

The thought of the Last Judgment holds an important place in the Qur'an. However, it is expressed seldom in the form of a theophany. The texts dealing with the "Coming of God" are very few. The reader has become acquainted with the main text quoted from some pages above. Generally, the question is about a "return" of man to God, whose presence may be surmised but who is not the object of a manifestation. The great majority of the texts dwell primarily on the division of men into two groups—the good and the wicked—and on their retribution. Sometimes we find a description of their respective destinies, but more frequently the purpose is to support a moral. This is a classical oratorical device: there is an anticipation of the future, and, in order to encourage the practice of the commandments, the awful punishment that will befall those who fail to obey is graphically described. The fear of hell is often emphasized in the Qur'an. Pious Muslims pray to be saved from everlasting fire. The attraction to paradise is there also, but less prominently.

Retribution shall be according to everyone's works. But what works are meant? The Qur'an insists strongly on charity to the poor (so also in the Epistle of St. James) and on kindness to the orphans (it should be remembered that Muhammad was an orphan at an early age). It also insists on a code of natural morals.

41

But gradually, as the opposition that confronted Muhammad became more definite and his pagan entourage accused him of falsifying, his message was rejected more bluntly and with greater boldness. Such obstinacy became one of the principal causes of damnation. There are many texts indeed saying that the *mokaddib* (one who accuses another of lying) is consigned into the everlasting fire!

In the beginning of this book, we spoke of the chronology of the different parts of the Qur'an. The preaching of those texts belongs to a period of twenty years. Some ideas were later more developed than they were at first; their importance, relative to the others, became more definite. In the present case, the doctrine of retribution according to one's works, the study of that evolution is most typical. Some points that were vague at first are clarified and made significant later on. As an example, we may take, among the oldest texts, 92:14–21:

> I have warned you of an intensely blazing fire that only the most wretched shall endure, who have accused of imposture and turned away from [the truth]. Removed away from it shall be the God-fearing man who gives his wealth endeavoring to be pure and holy, and [gives] to none any favor that should be rewarded, but seeks only the face of his Lord the Most High. And assuredly he shall be satisfied. [Compare, for the general idea, Mt 6:1–4.]

But gradually, as the struggle against the opponents became more intense, the chief importance came to be given to the confession of the unity of God, which was regarded as the principal good work:

> Allah witnesses, with the angels and the possessors of knowledge, that there is no God standing firm on justice equity but He; no God but He, the Mighty, the Wise. (3:16/18)

Without this confession and without the submission to the "signs" of Allah, that is, without acceptance of the whole message of the prophets as Islam sees it, therefore the resurrection, the Qur'an, and Muhammad, good works deserve no reward in the hereafter:

> Those who rejected [as impostures (*Kaddabu*)] our signs (*Ayyati*) and the coming [literally, meeting] of the hereafter, vain are their deeds. Shall they be rewarded, except for what they were doing? (7:145/147)

Again:

> If one rejects faith, vain is his work. In the hereafter, he will be one of the losers. (5:7/5)

Such a view would deserve close study. It shows that salvation depends first on faith. One cannot enter the Muslim heaven without faith. Muslim theologians have spoken of faith abundantly. They have asked whether faith was purely internal or necessarily involved public profession; or even if it must necessarily include works. In any case, Muslims see faith in a perspective that differs from that of Christians.

Faith is primarily *Tasdiq*, that is, acknowledging a statement as true. For others it is *Tasdiq* plus works.

Another point merits our attention. For the Qur'an, there is only one unforgivable sin, namely, associating other beings with God and considering them equal with Him:

> Verily God does not forgive one who sets up partners with Him, but He forgives anything else. If one sets up partners with God, indeed he devises a heinous sin. (4:41/48)

The Qur'an threatens with everlasting hell those who have committed various grievous sins, such as purposely killing a Muslim, and so forth. The verse on the unforgivable sin has often been compared with the verses on everlasting hell. In the case of unbelievers, Muslim exegesis has not run into difficulties: everything is very definite. Some thinkers have, however, appealed to phrases that allow salvation in the case of one who was not responsible morally. But the view that favors the damnation of non-Muslims is held most commonly. The case of a Muslim who sins grievously and is obstinate and acts deliberately presents a difficulty. Very few have insisted on the clause in 4:41/48, which says: "God forgives whom He wills", except in the case of the unforgivable sin of "associating partners with God". This clause could be taken to mean that God does not forgive always necessarily the obdurate Muslim sinner. Therefore, some may remain in hell everlastingly. In fact, almost unanimously (excepting the mo'tazilite school of theology) the Muslim view today is that hell will not be everlasting for the Muslim who confessed the unity of God. According to the Qur'an this was the view of the Jews who held that they would enjoy a special treatment:

> They said: The fire will not touch us except for a determined time [literally, for some numbered days]. Say: Have you received a covenant with God, for God never breaks His covenant, or do you say of God what you do not know? Nay, those who commit evil and whom their sins surround, they are companions of the fire; in it they shall live forever. And they who believe and do righteous things, these are the companions of the Garden; in it they shall live forever. (2:74–75/80–81)

10

Narratives Concerning Some Ancient Saints, Especially the Great Biblical Personages

Their number is considerable. They appear individually, in anecdotes, as examples quoted in preaching—not in the sequence of a large historical recital, but according to circumstances, to serve as lessons. They recall God's demands, His omnipotence, and the punishments sent by Him. They teach monotheism, the resurrection, and the mission of the prophets and messengers. They mention the Torah as given by God to Moses, the Psalms as given to David, the Gospel as given to Jesus. Most of them deal with the community of the "Children of Israel". We see the confidence of those holy personages who pray to God in a moving manner, as, for instance, Zechariah:

> He said: My Lord, indeed my bones are weak and my head has become shining with gray, but I have not been disappointed in my prayers to You, and now I fear [what] my relatives [will do] after me; my wife is barren, so give me from You an heir . . . and make him, my Lord, one pleasing [to You] . . . O Zachariya! We give you the good news of a boy [whose name shall be] Yahya. (19:3–5/4–5)

We find there also God's miracles and His covenants with Noah, Abraham, Moses, Jesus, and the Children of Israel, chosen by God especially. However, to understand that choice correctly, we must see it in the light of the Muslim religious history of the world. The choice is not exclusive or irrevocable.

The principal characters of these narratives are Adam and his wife, whose name is not given (but, in the Qur'an, no woman, except Mary, appears under her name); the two sons of Adam, Cain and Abel (though their names are not given); Idriss, Noah and his sons, Hud, Salih, Sho'ayb (three Arabian nonbiblical prophets); Abraham, Lot, Isaac, Ishmael, Jacob, Joseph, Moses, Aaron, Haman (as vizier of Pharaoh), Korah, Jalut and Talut (that is, Saul and Goliath), David and Solomon, Elijah, Job, Jonah, then the man with the two horns; Zechariah and his son (Yahya), Mary, daughter of 'Imran, elsewhere also called sister of Aaron (Harun), and the mother of Jesus, Jesus ('Isa), the people of the Cave (the seven sleepers of Ephesus).

The names of John the Baptist (Yahya) and of Jesus ('Isa) raise a problem. Their etymology is not clear.

We find these names in such a form among the Mandeans, who are a remnant of formerly flourishing "baptist" sects, but they may have been borrowed at a later date from Islam.

There are also stories about unknown or anonymous saints. Some refer to the jinns, how some became Muslims, or how some were stoned by shooting stars when they tried to listen to conversations in the upper heavens.

From the point of view of a comparison between the Bible and the Qur'an, these narratives may be divided into three groups:

1. *Accounts that occur in the Bible with some variants.* It should be noted that in the Qur'an there are no narratives in the exact wording of the Bible. What we find are sum-

maries, varying accounts on the same themes that preserve the essential thought.

2. *Accounts known only from rabbinic literature or apocryphal literature.*

3. *Other narratives.*

1. Accounts that occur in the Bible with some variants

These variants, minor as they may be, should be noted, as they point at times to a detail in the account in a special sense. (Thus, for instance, Abraham's immediate submission; he does not argue with God when he intercedes for Sodom; this serves to emphasize more strongly the transcendence of God.) Sometimes we discern in these narratives a literary device of the Qur'an (for example, anticipating what follows in the account when a character says what he expects to do; this is a dramatic amplification). Among the narratives of this class we may list the following themes: Adam's sin in paradise, the Flood, the tidings of a son to be born to Abraham in his old age (the son's name is not mentioned), Abraham's sacrifice, the destruction of Lot's city, and so forth, even the Annunciation, in which Mary's virginity is clearly affirmed (19:16ff.).

However, Moses is unquestionably the most outstanding Old Testament personage in the Qur'an. To him are given a large number of verses, and the texts of the Qur'an agree best with what the Pentateuch tells us about him.

As an illustration we can examine 20:37–50/37–48:

And indeed We bestowed upon you a favor another time [before]: When We revealed to your mother what was revealed: Cast [the child] into the ark [chest], and throw [the chest] into the river; the river will cast him back on the bank. One who is an enemy to Me and an enemy to him will take him, and I cast upon you love from Me [as a garment] so that you might be brought up under My eye. See, when your sister went and said: Shall I show you one who will take care of the child? So We took you back to your mother, in order that her eye might be refreshed and she should not grieve. And you killed a man, and We saved you from affliction, and We tried you with various trials, and you remained for years among the people of Midian. Then you came here as decreed, O Moses! And I appointed you for Myself [for service]. Go, you and your brother, with My signs (*ayyati*), and be not negligent in remembering Me. Go both of you to Pharaoh. Verily he is exceedingly wicked. But speak, both of you, to him mildly. He may fear [God]. They said: Our Lord! We fear lest he be insolent toward us or lest he behave very wickedly. He said: Be not afraid; I am with both of you. I hear and I see [all things].

So both of you go to him and say: Verily both of us are messengers of your Lord. So send with us the Children of Israel and do not afflict them. Indeed we have come to you from your Lord with Signs. And peace be on those who follow guidance!

Verily it has been revealed to us: The punishment is upon [awaits] those who reject (*kaddab*) and turn away.

2. *Accounts known only from rabbinic or apocryphal literature*

Most of these have been collected in a study that places in parallel form the rabbinic or apocryphal texts and their Qur'anic versions. The juxtaposition speaks for itself. These narratives tell, for instance, about the repentance and forgiveness of Adam, Noah's preaching to his people to warn them of the Flood, Solomon and the Queen of Sheba, and so forth. In that group we also find accounts concerning Mary's infancy, the episode of Jesus' speaking in the cradle to defend His mother's virginity, the miracle of the bird molded from clay, to which Jesus gave life.

Muslims receive these narratives as the Word of God, without inquiring about their historical background. In fact we have there a popular, poetic form of legends, variants of religious themes known from other sources. They help to recall those themes to the Muslim soul, as a golden legend would do, whatever may be the material historical value of the facts. They are, all of them, edifying tales.

The Qur'anic picture of Abraham presents some of the features that we find in Genesis, others that are mentioned in rabbinic literature, and, again, others that are specific to the Qur'an. In the Qur'an, Abraham is the defender of the unity of God; he fights against idolatry; he is the *hanif*, the holiest representative of natural religion. Compared with Genesis, the perspective is different. In Genesis the emphasis is on God's choice of Abraham and the blessing of his posterity; he worships only one God, but he is not going about challenging idolaters and smashing idols as Elijah will do later. He goes to Egypt, the land of pagan temples and idols, but he does not dispute with the people of the country. For the Bible, what we have with Abraham is a quite new dialogue between God and man, one that is quiet, without commotion, and that will end in the messianic revelation. In the Qur'an, Abraham is the perfect representative of the unchangeable natural religion. In Genesis he is the first patriarch of sacred history. He inaugurates a new stage in the development of mankind's religious history. The following text in the Qur'an will reveal one of the features of Abraham's picture in the rabbinic literature:

> See, he said to his father and his people: What are these statues to which you are so devoted?
>
> They said: We found our fathers worshipping them.
>
> He said: Indeed you and your fathers have been in manifest error.

They said: Have you come to us with the truth, or are you one of those who jest?

He said: Nay, your Lord is the Lord of the heavens and the earth, who created them, and I am one of those who testify to this [truth], and by God; I will contrive a stratagem against your idols after you will have turned your backs.

So he smashed them to pieces except the largest of them. Perhaps they might blame it for [the dead].

[On the return], [the people] said: Who has done this to our gods? Certainly some wicked man.

They said: We heard a youth called Abraham talk of them.

They said: Bring him before the people. Perhaps they may [be able] to bear witness.

They said: Did you do this to our gods, O Abraham?

He said: Nay, he did it, the largest one of them. Ask them, if they [can] speak.

So they came to their senses and said: It is you yourselves who are wrong.

Then they were confounded with shame and said: You know that these [statues] do not speak.

So said Abraham: Do you worship besides God [Allah] what is useful or harmful to you? Shame on you and on what you worship besides God. Do you then have no sense?

They said: Burn him and defend your gods if you are to do [anything]!

We [Allah] said: O Fire, be cool and a means of security for Abraham.

And they wanted [to devise] a stratagem against [Abraham].
But we made them the losers. (21:53–70/52–70)

The narrative just read is a lesson in monotheism. There
are, however, other types of Qur'anic (or rabbinic) narratives that take the reader to a form of poetry in which jinns
and marvelous facts are apparently called upon, chiefly to
satisfy imagination. They fill the gaps of the Bible and introduce us, in their own special way, to far more serious
ideas. Thus the legend and the deeds of Solomon and the
account of his death. God made the winds subservient to
Solomon, also the devils (21:81ff.). Solomon is given knowledge of the various voices of the birds (27:16). For his death,
see 34:11–13/12–14:

> When We decreed death for him, nothing revealed his death
> to them [the jinns] except that a creature of the earth [ter-
> mite] gnawed the staff; and [when Solomon, who had been
> leaning on the staff] fell down, the jinns realized [that Sol-
> omon was dead]. If [the jinns] had known the unknown,
> they would not have remained in that ignominious punish-
> ment [their task].

Such a narrative is interesting because it reveals a special
mentality. First, it teaches that the jinns have no divine power
of knowledge. The purpose is to extol God's transcendence.
Besides, in Solomon's material works, the Qur'an does not
praise human energy, but gives credit for them to the jinns.
Being in the service of their master, they only try to get out
of that hard work that is referred to as an ignominious punishment. Here we find attributed to the jinns a philosophy
of labor. We discern the repugnance of peoples for the co-
lossal undertakings of their kings, the burdens that such works
lay on ordinary persons (compare 1 Kings 12:4). There may
be also something of the nomad's contempt for the worker's

task, the worker being usually a man of servile condition or belonging to a tribe of a lower rank.

3. *Other narratives*

Some are about unknown prophets of ancient Arabia, for instance, Salih, the prophet of the people of Thamood. He warned his people against disobedience. He commanded them to save a sacred she-camel, but they slaughtered the beast, and their rebellion led to their destruction. This is an etiological legend that explains the ruins of ancient buildings near which the trading caravans of the Meccan merchants use to pass.

Others form a cycle in which Abraham appears as the founder of the Ka'ba (the temple at Mecca).

Still others introduce, in the guise of parables, historical personages; as, for instance, the parable of the garden destroyed by a tornado, because its owner, looking forward to a rich harvest, neglected to leave the matter in the hands of Providence.

The Qur'an, a Book of Apologetics

The Qur'an includes many polemical sections. It is a witness to the Meccan pagans' objections. It records them and replies to them. It puts forward a series of arguments. In some ways it is a veritable book of apologetics, which defends the essential points of its very simple message.

The doctrine of the resurrection was the first item to which the pagans of Mecca took exception. The Meccans cried out that this was a lie. In reply, the Qur'an at times merely repeated the doctrine; for a repeated statement emphasized with great oratorical force is a means of shaking and impressing the minds of the hearers:

> Your many rivalries engross your attention until the time comes to visit the burial place. Well then, you will see! . . . Nay, if you could only know certainly! And I say to you: You will see the flaming Furnace. Then, that day you will be questioned about [your] pleasures. (102:7–8)

As the objections become urgent, the Qur'an replies:

> The unbelievers say: This is an extraordinary thing. What! Once we are dead, we are dust, that is a return far [from understanding or possibility]. (50:2–3)

Hence the Qur'an does not merely affirm; it strives to convince by appealing to arguments.

The fact that there will be a resurrection depends on God and is not to be proved. But its possibility may be maintained. Thus we find in the Qur'an reasons *ex convenientia*, such as were used by the Fathers of the Church in the second century in their controversies with the pagans. They are based on the power of God, who, since He created the world a first time, can make a "second creation". He, who by sending the rain returns life to the dry desert, can again give life to the dead. Finally, He who formed the embryo in its mother's womb will have no difficulty in rebuilding the human body. It should be noted that this latter argument appears in far more delicate terms in 2 Maccabees 7:23–24:

> The Creator of the world, who shaped the beginning of man and devised the origin of all things, will in his mercy give life and breath back to you again, since you now forget yourselves for the sake of his laws.

The most complete text of this Qur'anic apologetics occurs in 22:5–6:

> O Man, if you are in doubt about the resurrection, [so remember] that We created you from dust, then from a life-germ (cf. 16:4), then from clotted blood, then from a lump of flesh, [partly] formed and [partly] unformed, in order that We may manifest [Our power] to you, then We cause to rest [or remain] in the wombs what We will until the appointed term; then We bring you out as infants in order that you may reach your age of full strength; then of you there are some who die, and of you there are some who are kept back [sent back] to the most feeble age of life so that they do not know [anything] after they have known [much]. And you see the earth barren and lifeless, but when We send down water upon it, it stirs itself and swells and puts forth [growth] of every beautiful [plant] couple. This is because God is the

Truth [Reality]. He gives life to the dead, and He has power over everything.

The pagan opposition was not limited to a criticism of the doctrine of the bodily resurrection. It extended also to the person of Muhammad. He was accused of lying (*kaddab*), [of forging] revelations that he had learned from a man; he was a mad [possessed] poet or soothsayer, whose views will destroy the traditional religion:

> They say you are only a forger (*muftir*). Indeed, we know that they say: It is only a man that teaches him. But the language of him to whom they are referring maliciously is barbarous; but this is clear Arabic language. (16:101 ff.)

> Verily this is the word of a respected messenger (*rasul*) and not the word of a poet. It is a revelation from the Lord of the worlds. Surely they behave insolently when it was said to them: There is no God but God [Allah], and they said: Shall we leave our gods for a possessed poet? (37:34–35/36–37)

The Qur'an discusses, argues, in order to prove that God is One. Sometimes the argument starts from the unity that may be observed in the created world, and thence it rises to the unity of the Creator:

> If there were in heavens and on the earth gods besides Allah, [the heavens and the earth] would be in a state of confusion. But, Glory to God, the Lord of the throne, high above what they assert. (21:22)

As will be seen more clearly in chapter 12, the Qur'an's view of the unity of God excludes the divine sonship of Jesus and the Trinity:

> Allah has not taken to Himself a son, and there is no other god with Him. Else each god would have gone with what

he had created, and [the one or the other] would be above. Glory to God above what they ascribe to Him. (23:93/91)

When speaking of the pagans who ascribe female divinities to God as daughters, the Qur'an uses irony. The Bedouins are bitterly disappointed when they hear that their wives have given birth to girls. And they imagine that God has daughters!

When one of them is told of [the birth of] a daughter, his face becomes black, as he is grieving in silence. He hides himself from the people because of the bad news he has received. [He thinks] shall he keep the child [with disgrace] or bury[1] [literally, hide] [the child] in the dust? (16:59–61/57–59)

To Muhammad's mind, birth and generation are something sexual that cannot be imagined in God's case:

How can He have a son as He has no consort? (6:101/102)

The other so-called gods associated with the One true God have created nothing; they are powerless, cannot help or save, are unable to prevent God from giving favors to whom He wills, unable to prevent God from bringing about the evil He has resolved to send. The Qur'an appeals to the pagan's religious feeling. In danger, they invoke the One God and forget the false gods; then when the danger has passed, they go back to their errors. Indeed the pagans of Mecca believe in one greater God (Allah, in Arabic), the Creator of heaven and earth, but they associate with Him lower gods and revel in this form of worship:

[1] This refers to the custom, among ancient Arabs, of burying newborn daughters. Maulvi Muhammad Ali in *The Holy Qur'an* (p. 645) mentions the abolition of this custom as one of the great achievements of Islam.

> If you ask them who created heaven and earth and controls the sun and the moon, they say Allah. (29:61)

This kind of polemics against the false divinities is rather common in the Qur'an. It is in the same line as that of the prophets of Israel against the idols of Palestine, except that it is more didactic. We might find something like it in the Jewish and Christian apologetic literature. For instance, the Judeo-Christians of the Pseudo-Clementines frequently debate with pagans. It would be interesting to follow in detail the arguments of some of those debates. We would see that one of the names of the One God, *al-Rahman* (the compassionate one), was definitely rejected by the people of Mecca. This was due perhaps to the circumstance that the One God was worshipped under that name by strict monotheistic groups in South Arabia, where Jewish and Christian inscriptions mention God under the name *Rahman*, or rather *Rahmanan*, which is its South Arabic equivalent. On the other hand, the name "Allah" was originally used in Arabian circles that accepted secondary deities:

> When it is said to them: Adore *al-Rahman*, they say: And who is *al Rahman*? Shall we adore at your command?, and this increases [their] distaste. (25:61/60)

One of the objections mentioned in several places is the fact that Muhammad wrought no miracle to support his claim. A pagan hearing his preaching finds in it only tales of the Ancients (68:15). As we saw above, he was accused of being helped by a foreigner who spoke barbarous Arabic, and he replied by saying that the language of the Qur'an is clear Arabic. Such a reply deals only with the form of the language but ignores the question of the thought and the possibility of some help from one who would have transmitted those "tales" to the Prophet. The reply thus has some force only for one who already believes in the Qur'an as the Word of God. For a Muslim, naturally, to entertain such a possibility would be a sin.

Indeed, as we have seen before, it is the literary form, the originality of which cannot be denied, that will become the great argument. The claim that the Qur'an is inimitable is for the Muslims a miracle that proves its divine origin.

The reader may compare such a view with the case of the Bible. There are, of course, passages of exceptional beauty of form, but the authors do not appeal to that feature as an argument for the divine origin of the Bible. This insistence on the literary value of the Qur'an as an apologetic argument is something peculiarly Muslim.

Considering the inimitability, we should bear in mind the fact that any great work of art is in some way inimitable. The object of art is to produce something original, individual. Every artistic creation has its special characteristics that distinguish it from other works. But Christians, while recognizing and admiring literary beauty, realize that this, of itself, is insufficient as part of a proof of divine origin. The Qur'anic apologetics is not convincing to them on this point.

We find also in the Qur'an echoes of the polemics between the Muslims and the Medinan Jews, before the latter were driven out by force. However, the lack of documents prevents any detailed reconstruction of the history of that period. It is likely that it began when the Muslims realized that the Jews did not agree with their presentation of the Bible and noted points of disagreement.

In any case, the Qur'an, not indeed in the very beginning, but after several months of Judeo-Muslim coexistence in Medina, attacks those it calls the "people of the Book" in general, the Jews especially.

At first we find entreaties, appeals to the faith, presenting the Jews' refusal of Islam as ingratitude for the many favors of God to Israel. The situation, as suggested by the following verses, is still bearable, but there is bitterness in the last sentence:

Children of Israel, remember My favor that I bestowed upon you, and fulfill the covenant with Me, [as] I fulfill the covenant with you. Fear Me and believe in what I have sent down [revealed to Muhammad]; it confirms [the revelation] that you have [already]; be not the first to disbelieve and do not barter My revelations for a mean price. Fear Me and do not obscure truth with falsehood, nor conceal the truth knowingly. Perform the prayer and give the poor-tax and bow down [in worship] with those who bow down. (2:38–39/40–42)

The same conclusion follows when we take note of another verse that says that Jews, Christians and Sabians (probably members of baptist sects) will be saved if they follow the precepts of their respective faiths as they are understood by the Qur'an:

Those who believe [in the Qur'an] and those who practice Judaism, and the Christians and the Sabians, all who believe in God, in the Last Day and in the good works, shall have their reward with the Lord; among them shall be no fear, and they shall suffer no disgrace. (2:59/62)

Soon, however, the outlook for Judeo-Muslim relations was to become darker. Later, the preceding verse was either abrogated or simply understood as applying to a Judaism or Christianity that differed greatly from the orthodox tradition and accepted Islam. For in Islam there is an exegetical tradition based on some clear texts of the Qur'an. The doctors of Muslim Law refer to this point frequently; certain

verses are abrogated by the Qur'an itself and replaced by other
verses:

> We do not abrogate [any] of Our revelations or cause them
> to be forgotten without bringing something better or like it.
> Do you not know that God has all power? (2:100/106)

The Qur'an blames the Jews for their attitude of ambig-
uous expectancy. They themselves feel that the Muslims are
taking advantage of them since at that time the Muslims
learned about the Bible from the Jews. The Qur'an replies
by accusing them of tampering with the text of Scripture:

> See, when they meet the believers, they say: We believe. But
> when they are among themselves they say: Are you going to
> tell them what God has revealed to you so that they may
> dispute with you about it before your Lord?
>
> Will you not understand [their purpose?] or do they re-
> alize that God knows what they conceal and what they
> publish?
>
> Some of them, illiterates, do not know the Book [Scrip-
> ture] but only stories and conjectures.
>
> Woe to them who write the Book [Scripture] with their
> hands, then say: This is from God, in order that they may
> make a small profit by it. And woe to them ... for their
> profit. (2:71–73/76–79)

The attacks become more and more bitter. The Qur'an
recalls how the Children of Israel were disobedient to God
throughout their history. They killed people among themselves, banished people from their homes, put to death the
prophets of God:

> Then you yourselves kill people of yours, drive some of your
> people from their houses ... slay the prophets of God.
> (2:85/91)

The Jews and Christians will have no regard for Muhammad before he becomes one of them, a thing that is impossible for the Prophet who has received the revelation.

And the Jews and Christians will not find you acceptable before you follow their religion. Say, verily, the guidance of Allah is the guidance; and if you follow their desires, after receiving the knowledge, you shall have no protector, nor helper from Allah. Those to whom we have given the Book and who follow it as they should, these believe in it, and those who disbelieve in it, these are the losers. (2:114/120)

Islam now begins to consider itself as a religion, distinct from Judaism and Christianity:

They say: Be Jews or Christians, you will be guided aright. Say, O Muhammad, No! [We follow] the religion of Abraham as a *hanif* [a holy representative of natural religion]; he was not one of the polytheists [literally, associators]. (2:129/135)

The whole cycle of Abraham regarded as a founder of the Meccan worship is now brought out. The Qur'an does not accept the idea that the Jews and Christians possess a specially favored place in God's plan, which Islam would not enjoy:

And the Jews and the Christians said: We are the sons of God and His beloved ones. Say: Why then does He punish you for your sins? No! you are [just] creatures of His. He forgives whom He wills and punishes whom He wills. To Allah belongs the kingdom of heaven and earth and what is between them. (5:21/18)

Then it was that the internal logic of Islam showed itself in the most evident manner. Total submission to God was not enough; it was to be accompanied by complete obedience to the Qur'an and to the Prophet. Such an attitude was normal. Once one is recognized as a messenger of God, full submission to God demands that one should follow His messenger and obey the message that he brings. Note also in the preceding verse an idea that was destined to have great importance in the history of the relations between the Muslims, on the one hand, and the Jews and Christians, on the other.

Success is given as the sign of God's blessing. Strictly speaking, there are in the Qur'an verses that present the temporary trials of the Muslims (the defeat at Uhud, March 625, the hardships of the military campaigns, and so forth) as willed by God and as sources of future rewards. Nevertheless, the thought of the Qur'an generally is that the truth of Islam was manifested by force and victory, notably at Badr (April 624). In the case referred to in the preceding verse, the fact that the Jews and the Christians have to suffer is presented as a sign of a divine rejection. The Qur'an does not have those long developments found in the Bible that explain that suffering may be a temporal chastisement sent by God in order to bring His people back to the right way. Islam, bound to an apologetics of force and victory, apparently does not share that attitude. This may be so because such ideas are intelligible only from the point of view of love, and love does not lower one; rather it is sin alone that debases.

In short, from the very first years of Muhammad's life in Medina, a conflict between the Muslims and the other two groups appeared to be unavoidable. The presence of a strong group of Orthodox Jews in that city hastened the crisis. The illusions vanished, and this spelled the end.

With the Christians, the situation remained uncertain for a longer time. It was still so at Muhammad's death. The first Muslims had no direct knowledge of any strongly organized Orthodox Christian community. In Arabia itself, what were the sects to which the Christians belonged and with whom the Muslims came into contact? It is hard to know. Hence, the Qur'an does not reproduce against the Christians the equivalent of the arguments ad hominem, the entreaties, the accusations, the insinuations that are used against the Jews. The Qur'an merely defines the doctrine more clearly: God has no son because He has no consort; Christ is not God, because he had a human body subject to the same physiological functions as other men, for instance, eating and drinking; Muslims must not speak of three in connection with God, and so forth.

Conversions to Islam seem to have been more numerous among those Christians of Arabia than among the Jews. In April 627, in Medina, on the occasion of the slaughter of six hundred or nine hundred men of a Jewish Arabian tribe (the Qorayza), only four of them saved their lives by accepting Islam, which was offered to them. Hence, a passage of the Qur'an speaks of the Christians more favorably than of the Jews. The Christians are said to be closer to Islam than the Jews.

> Certainly, the Jews and the polytheists, you [Muhammad] will find most bitterly opposed to the believers, and you will find closest in friendship to the believers those who say: We are Christians. This is because there are priests among them, and monks, and they do not act proudly. And when they hear what has come down [been revealed] to the messenger, you see their eyes overflowing with tears for what they know of the truth. They say: Our Lord, inscribe us with those who witness [to the truth]. (5:85–86/82–83)

The significance of these two verses will be clear to everyone. We have here a judgment on the closeness of the Muslims and the Christians. This closeness is proved by the

conversion of Christians to Islam. Moreover, the fact that
they are not behaving proudly means—as the expression is
used in the Qur'an—that they do not oppose the signs and
the worship of God, therefore that they follow God's prophets. The tradition of the commentators has emphasized the
circumstance that here the question was about Christians becoming converts to Islam. The two verses, therefore, refer to
Christians who are accepting the faith of Islam or are in-
clined to do so. These are the Christians to whom the sympathy of the Muslims goes out.

Still we should not restrict the sense to this particular case.
Even today, Muslims who wish to show sympathy to Christian friends often quote this text, up to the words about priests
and monks not behaving proudly. This text does not speak
of the fundamental legislative positions of Islam regarding
Christianity. But in any case the verse has significance by
itself.

To the Muslim, every sentence of the Qur'an conveys a
lesson that the believer must put into practice. Every sentence has a hold on him, thanks to its rhythm, its fascination,
and especially because he hears in it the very Word of God.
This verse is an overture at least at the individual level. It
enables one to start personal contacts, and this is quite
important.

I2

Jesus in the Qur'an

This chapter, as the reader will note, follows the chapter entitled "The Qur'an, a Book of Apologetics".

This is because the Qur'an presents the person of Christ under a twofold aspect. On the one hand, the Qur'an speaks of Jesus with great respect; several statements suggest His holiness very clearly. But on the other hand, the Qur'an mentions Jesus in an apologetic context to show that He is just a mere creature. The subject is immense, and we cannot treat it here as fully as might be wished. It has been studied exhaustively in a number of publications and from many different standpoints. We can give here only some indications that may guide the reader. We should not forget, however, that the Qur'an is very respectful toward Jesus and that Muslims have a high veneration for the person of Christ as presented to them by the Qur'an.

The human characteristics of Jesus, as the Qur'an describes them, are manifold. Jesus and Mary, His mother, are spoken of as being of exceptional purity. The Qur'an calls Mary's father 'Imran (thus the same name as that of the father of Moses, Aaron, and Miriam, their sister, in the Bible, with the difference that in the Bible the name ends with the letter "m" instead of "n"). When Mary's mother was expecting her child, she vowed to God the child to be born. She gave birth to a girl. But the Qur'an refers to a boy to whom the birth would lead finally, for indeed the

person of Mary and that of Jesus cannot be separated in the
Qur'an:

> [Recall] when the wife of 'Imran said: My Lord, I vow to
> You what is in my womb as devoted [to Your service]. So
> receive it from me. Verily, You are the One who hears, the
> One who knows.
>
> When she brought forth [her child], she said: My Lord,
> verily I have brought forth a girl [God knew well what she
> had brought forth. The male is not like a girl] and I have
> called her Mary [Maryam] and I place her in your care and
> her offspring against the accursed devil.
>
> And so her Lord accepted the child graciously. (3:31/35-36)

A few verses farther on, we read:

> The angels said: O Mary, God has chosen and purified you.
> He has chosen you above the women of the world. (3:37/41)

The phrase of the Qur'an: "I place her in your care and
her offspring against the accursed devil" has been closely studied by Muslim doctors. In the most respected collections of
Muslim traditions it is recorded that Satan touches all the
children of men at their birth. Their wailing then is the sign
of it. Mary and Jesus alone have been preserved from that
unclean touch:

> Abu Huraira says: I heard the messenger of God say: No de-
> scendant of Adam is born but that Satan touches him at birth,
> except Mary and her son Jesus. (Bokhari, *Book of the Proph-
> ets*, no. 44; Moslim, *Book of the Virtues*)

The outlook of Islam is rather different from that of Christianity. What is the meaning of that touch of Satan? Islam
does not know the doctrine of original sin, and here the
question is about the birth, not the conception. Besides, Satan's touch comprises also temptation, according to some au-

thors. Personally we prefer not to carry the comparison between Christianity and Islam too far on the question of Mary's purity. Else we are in danger of applying to Islam an elaborate vocabulary of Christian theology. It will be enough to say, while emphasizing the importance of such an affirmation, that in Islam Mary is the "Immaculate". When Sisters speak of Mary's purity to young Muslim girls, their words find a deep echo in the souls of those young hearers.

Mary remained a virgin, according to the Qur'anic account of the Annunciation and some other verses. She is an example to those who believe:

> And God has set forth an example to those who believe: the wife of Pharaoh when she said: My Lord, build for me near You a dwelling in the Garden and save me from the Pharoah and his doing, and save me from the wicked people. [He also offered the example of] Mary the daughter of 'Imran who preserved her chastity. So We breathed into [her] some of Our Spirit and she declared true the words of her Lord and His books and she was one of those obedient to God [or constant in prayer]. (66:11–12)

See also 21:91:

> And we made her and her son a sign for the world.

This purity is also a characteristic that the Qur'an acknowledges in Jesus. The Qur'an has many prophets who ask God's forgiveness and who are told by God that their sins are forgiven. The Qur'an does not refer to sins in the case of Christ. Hence many Sufis [Muslim mystics] look upon Jesus as a great model of holiness. Among the people, as far as we can know through Egyptian testimonies, it is especially Jesus' miracles that attract their attention. In the Qur'an, Jesus was born without a human father; this the commentators compare with Adam's creation, Adam without father or mother. Jesus healed the sick, brought the dead back to life. Among the miracles we have also the words spoken by the newborn child to those who doubted His mother's virginity; also the miracle of the bird modeled from clay to which He gave life (miracles mentioned in the apocryphal Gospels of the Infancy).

The Qur'an makes it clear that all this was done with "God's permission". The commentators insist on that clause in order to point out that Jesus was a creature who acted through the power of God. However, they note that the miraculous facts of Jesus' life are to be found also in the lives of other prophets, including His being raised to heaven by God, whence He shall return at the end of time to complete His earthly life and die. His return will be a time of complete peace, as believed by the advocates of the millennium. Whatever view one may take of the commentators' explanations, it remains that even according to the Qur'an Jesus is the only prophet around whom so many miracles are collected; besides, the miracle of the return is His alone. Again, according to the Qur'an, Jesus received the Gospel and gathered disciples about Him. At their request, He asked God to send down from heaven a table set out with food. Hence the name *al-Ma'ida* (the table, the food) given to surah 5. This mysterious table has been understood as an allusion to the miracle of the multiplication of the loaves, or to the Last Supper, the real sense of which remains obscure to the Muslim commentators.

Jesus was very highly regarded in this world and will be very highly regarded also in the next. The commentators explain this as due to Jesus' gift of miracles and the power of His intercession in the next world. As a messenger to the Children of Israel, He abrogated some juridical prescriptions of the Torah:

[God] will teach him the Book (*Kitab*) and wisdom, and the Torah, and the Gospel (*Injil*) . . . messenger (*rasul*) to the Children of Israel. . . . I have come to you with a sign from your Lord. I make from the clay [something] like the form of a bird, and I breathe into it, and it will be a [living] bird with the permission of God. And I heal the blind from birth, and the leper, and I raise the dead, with the permission of God, verifying what was [revealed] before me of the Torah, to allow to you part of what was forbidden. (3:48/50)

These texts show the great respect of the Qur'an for Jesus and His mother. Still it is not easy for us Christians to see clearly the place that Muslims give to Jesus in actual life.

The texts of the Qur'an that speak of Jesus are materially far less extensive than those that deal with the great Qur'anic themes. One may listen to the broadcasts of many Muslim sermons and hear no mention of Jesus. The speakers may refer to him on the occasion of a political event or of some festival of special interest to Christians. Muslims like to speak of Him to their Christian friends. But, when they are among themselves, what happens? After they have expressed their faith in Jesus as in all the prophets, the rest is apparently a matter of private devotion, which will take on various forms according to individuals.

Also we must not forget that the Qur'an states very definitely that Jesus is only a creature. It rejects clearly the mystery of the Incarnation. This appears evident from the restrictive particle used in the following text:

[Jesus] is nothing but a servant on whom We bestowed favor. We made Him an example for the Children of Israel. (43:59)

It is not right for a man to whom God gives the Book (*Kitab*), a rule [power], and the office of prophet, that he should say

to the people: Be my servants instead of God's servants! . . .
God would not tell you to take angels and prophets as mas-
ters. (3:73–74/79–80)

For Islam, there is God, on the one hand, and all creatures,
on the other. The thought that God could have become incarnate and, while remaining what He is, appear to men veiled
by a human nature to which He is united seems excluded by
an intransigent idea of God's unity and transcendence.

The many apologetic texts that the Qur'an devoted to Jesus and His mother are on a plane that is not ours, that of a
universal idea of God, apart from the world of creation. As
the Qur'an directed its message in the first place against the
gods of paganism, with their stories of the birth of gods, it is
absolutely opposed to the idea of generation in God, for it
sees that generation in a sexual form; a form that, it hardly
needs to be said, is rejected by Christians just as emphatically.

The fullest text about Jesus is the following:

O People of the Book, be not exaggerated [go beyond the
proper limits] in your religion; do not utter [lies] against God,
but speak the truth. The Messiah, Jesus the son of Mary, is
only a messenger (*rasul*) of God, His word (*Kalimah*), which
He sent down to Mary and a Spirit from Him. Therefore,
believe in God [Allah] and His messengers and do not say
Three! Desist. It is better for you. God [Allah] is only One.
Far be it from Him that He should have a son! To Him belongs what is in the heavens and on the earth. God is suffi-
cient for a Protector. (4:169–70/171–72)

This appeal is addressed to Christians. The text might possibly be understood in a Christian sense, if one would scru-
tinize the interpretation of some terms. We have here two
great titles of Jesus: Messiah, Word of God. But in view of
the whole Qur'anic context, Muslims logically interpret this

text as a denial of the divinity of Jesus. "Do not say Three!" This absolute general statement is applied by the commentators to the Christian Trinity, which the Qur'an does not mention. The Qur'an refers to a Triad: Allah, Jesus, and Mary, which is not orthodox Christian doctrine. Muslims, who do not realize the real significance of the term "Messiah", see in the word a title of honor given to Jesus. So also the expression "Word" does not convey to Muslims the theological meaning of the term. The Spirit, conceived as a creature in the Qur'an, is an angel or a being higher than the angels, as some heterodox Judeo-Christians thought of Jesus.

In this verse we have the essential point of the difficulty. The high titles that the Qur'an gives to Jesus, if their full implications were understood properly, might be taken as remnants of an earlier revelation—guideposts that, if followed faithfully, might enable one to proceed in the right direction toward the light, in which one could see the real meaning of the title "Word of God", given to Christ in the Qur'an.

But, for the time being, categorical statements prevent any advance. The idea that religion is completely perfected with Islam, that the Qur'an has everything necessary to salvation (16:91/89), and the affirmation that Jesus is only a creature (43:59) are brought out by Muslims to justify their position.

True, Jesus is also called "the Word" (*Kalimah*), but this expression is used only twice. So also the word "Spirit", which occurs in different places but with different shades of meaning. The Christology of Islam from the very beginning is rather like that of the Judeo-Christians who looked upon Jesus as a prophet in the chain of the prophets sent by God to restore the natural religion with its belief in God, Creator and Providence, who will sanction the conduct of everyone with the favor of paradise or the punishment of hell.

Jesus' place in the Qur'anic plan of salvation confirms the statement just made. According to the Qur'an's teaching, salvation comes directly from God. With its uncompromising individualism, Islam maintains that each soul is responsible only for its own acts and that no one can help it on the Day of Judgment, except some privileged persons like Muhammad who have received from God the favor of interceding for others.

The principle of individual responsibility, so clearly stated by the prophet Ezekiel, is taken up again as a leitmotiv. Even if a soul wanted to redeem itself with all earthly treasures, it could not do so.

Islam does not take into account that there is on earth, besides the individual responsibility of everyone, a solidarity in suffering and atoning for sins. Islam is opposed to any idea of sacrifice, mediation; it brings forward the ever-repeated objection that God does not need all this in order to forgive; it forgets that there may be at times pedagogical reasons that make God ask from man what He does not need Himself, beginning with praise.

And without attempting to examine the consequences that, in Christian theology, flow from the unique place of Jesus, incarnate Word, true God and true man, Islam rejects altogether all idea of redemption.

Only one modern Muslim sect, which carries out propaganda in Europe (the Ahmadiyya), but which the traditional Muslim sects attack from time to time, admits that Jesus was really crucified. However, it holds that He was not dead when He was taken from the cross; He is supposed to have regained consciousness and to have gone to India, where He was buried finally. This sect, however, denies the doctrine of the Redemption just as definitely as the others.

The popular character of this book has compelled us to make a selection among the texts and to state our positions in a schematic form. It may be objected that the last expositions depend too much on Muslim commentators. Indeed, some Christians advocate the view that an effort should be made to interpret the key texts of the Qur'anic Christology in a purely Christian light, in order to show better all the resources that might be found there. As isolated texts easily suffer an interpretation when taken out of their context, they think that such an undertaking is justified. But, at present, we personally do not think that we have the right to do so. One fact impresses us: to millions of believers, the Qur'an means "Gospel of Salvation", quite distinct from ours, and it presents itself as complete in its line. They understand the general teaching of the Qur'an literally and see Christology in its light.

Nevertheless, it remains true that it suffices to see reality without illusions; and to avoid the risk of mutual offense, it is better to look afterward for the points on which we are in agreement.

We share in common with Muslims the wish to obey God's will fully and the wish to say nothing that may go against reason, even if at times revelation transcends our natural power; we believe in the Unity of God, in the fact that He spoke through the prophets. This is indeed much.

Perhaps one of the more important points will be found in the explanation of the message of Christ as it has been really transmitted to His disciples. When our positions on the authenticity of the Bible and the authenticity of its interpretation are understood, many obstacles in the way of a dialogue will disappear. Thus the problem of the authenticity of the Bible remains for the present a crucial problem in the question of the relations between Christians and Muslims.

13

Muslim Law

The Qur'an is also a Law book. In this it is similar to several books of the Old Testament. From the Muslim standpoint, even though salvation is obtained primarily through faith, which is the *conditio sine qua non* for admission to paradise, it is nevertheless true that the life of the community is regulated by very precise prescriptions and that works will be sanctioned on the Day of Judgment.

We know the place held by the lawyers and doctors of the Law in Islam. The Law of the Qur'an has also played a great part in the spread of Islam. The authorization of polygamy up to four simultaneous wives, the right to have women slaves, and the possibility of divorce were taken into account by many new converts. The regulation of mixed marriages allowed to Muslim men alone—not to Muslim women—and, moreover, for marrying women from the People of the Book (Jewish and Christian especially), and the rules on inheritance also have had their influence. These prescriptions are found in the Qur'an. Other regulations, such as those concerning apostasy, are later than the Qur'an, which only specifies the temporal chastisement of the traitors who turn back in that period of ceaseless wars.

We cannot deal with all these topics in detail. However, on this point, a comparison with the Old and New Testaments would be very instructive.

The Qur'an does not speak often of the love of God. It speaks primarily of His unity, of His knowledge, of His power, of His goodness and forgiveness. However, there are texts on the love of God. Many mystics (Sufis) have meditated on those verses as well as on the texts about the unity of God. Thus for instance:

> O You who believe! If anyone among you leaves his religion, God will bring a people whom He loves and who will love Him, humble toward believers, haughty toward unbelievers, who will fight in the Way of God, who will not fear the blame of anyone [literally, of those who find fault]. (5:57/54)

But the Qur'an refers rather often to God's love in connection with moral life. God loves those who do good, who are righteous, and so forth. He does not love the wicked, those who break the law, and so forth. This brings out the aspect of the kind, merciful Lord, who loves His faithful servants.

Muslim Law includes a moral code that in many ways reminds us of the precepts of natural law in the Decalogue. The rule is to do good and avoid evil; the Qur'an specifies which actions are good and which are evil. Muslim Law also includes positive precepts of rather varied character.

Indeed, the Qur'an contains many precepts for organizing the social life of the first Muslim community and for solving the practical difficulties that confronted it. The prescriptions concern both spiritual and temporal matters, the Muslim religion presenting itself as a religion both spiritual and temporal.

In Mecca, as early as between 612 and 622, the Qur'anic texts had regulated certain things to be done or not to be done, especially regarding moral life, prayer, almsgiving, adultery, respect for parents, asking forgiveness for sins, and so forth. In Medina, the organization of the theocratic community was the occasion of formulating the elements of a legislation (rules of purification, of foods, marriage, inheritance, Ramadan fast, pilgrimage, treatment of enemies in war, spoils, booty, and so forth). The texts are too numerous to be quoted here. We can give only an illustration. Thus:

> O You who believe, when you are praying [preparing for prayer], wash your face and your hands, [and arms] to the elbow, and rub your head and [wash] your feet to the ankles; and if you are ceremonially unclean, purify yourselves; and if you are ill, or on a journey, or if one of you comes from the privy place, or have touched women, and you do not find water, so use good sand and rub your face and hands; God does not wish to impose on you a difficult [obligation], but He wishes to make you clean and to complete His favor to you. Maybe you will be grateful. (5:8–9/6)

Some verses deal even with matters of courtesy, such as how to behave in the presence of the Prophet, so as not to be importunate:

> O You who believe, do not raise your voices above the voice of the Prophet; do not speak aloud to him as you do among yourselves, lest your [good] deeds become vain without your realizing it. (49:2–5)

> O You who believe, when you consult the Messenger privately, send before [it something] as alms; this will be better for you and more pure [?] [more decent]. If you do not do so [or, if you do not find the means], surely God is forgiving and merciful. Are you afraid of sending alms before your interview? If you do not do so, and God relents toward you, then fulfill the prayer and give the poor-tax and obey God and His Messenger. God knows quite well what you do. (58:13–14/12–13)

Regarding the status of non-Muslims, it should be noted that a difference is made between the people of the Book and the polytheists; for example, in the possibilities of marriage or for the payment of a tribute of protection, although here there is some discussion. Such statutes rests on a juridical distinction independent of the personal faith of those people of the Book. All Christians enjoy that protection under Islam, whether or not they believe in the divinity of Christ.

Purity is the dominant thought in all that legislation. Although this is not frequently expressed, it is one of the essential thoughts of the Qur'an. The Muslim community is a community of pure [clean] members.

> It is He who has sent among the *Ummi*[1] a messenger (*rasul*) from among themselves who recites to them His signs, purifies them, and teaches them the Book and wisdom. Verily, before they were in manifest error. (62:2)

What purity is meant? Legal purity or cleanliness, evidently; however, also interior purity. The Qur'an speaks of it in connection with some good deeds, such as almsgiving, that purify the soul. This notion of interior purity finds ready admittance in the Muslim soul. Even now, in Arabian countries, to refer to a man without sins, one says, "His heart is white."

A comparison with the Bible on this subject would require too much space. One could establish a parallel with the Mosaic Law. One could also compare the place of law in Christianity and in the Muslim economy of salvation.

---

[1] As stated before, the meaning of the word *Ummi* is disputed: illiterate, unlettered, one without a Scripture or revealed Book, etc.

14

Muslim Brotherhood

In 1958, the French review *La Vie spirituelle* published the notes of a priest who had spent a long time in the Sahara. He confessed that his contact with Muslims had led him to change his views on some points. He had hoped to find in them the sense of God, and he found it; but he soon discovered its limitations. However, he confessed that he had found the Muslim "brotherhood". The tone of his notes seemed to indicate that he had not suspected before the strength or appeal of that brotherhood for one who passes as a guest.

Yet, brotherhood is one of the most striking sociological realities of the Muslim world. This is, perhaps, because the great majority of Muslims are poor people, and poverty draws people closer together. But this is not enough to explain the phenomenon. We must go back to the Qur'an.

Before Islam (and it is still so), Bedouin law was based on tribal brotherhood. At a time of danger, all formed one unit to defend their common rights. The struggle for life in the desert, more than anywhere else, demands union. The traveler, the lone man, must be able to count on hospitality. Normally, such hospitality extends for three days, during which the guest receives food and protection under what is known as the "salt covenant". Woe to him who is alone! Never was this text of Scripture more true than in those immense arid stretches of land; and hospitality is a great virtue in the desert.

The Qur'an alludes to those customs frequently enough, but it shows how insufficient they are. Force and clan are helpless before God. Hence, in several ways the Qur'an modified the law of the desert. It established brotherhood on large bases: the Muslim community has become a unity within which relations analogous to those of tribes or clans are formulated.

The temporary unification of the Arab groups that lived in a state of permanent semi-hostility represents in Muhammad's work something that without doubt strongly impressed his contemporaries:

> And hold firmly by the bond [literally, rope] of God, be not divided among yourselves, and remember the favor of God on you: when you were enemies He united your hearts, and you became brothers by His favor; and you were on the brink of the pit of fire, and He saved you from it. Thus does God manifest to you His signs, that perhaps you may be guided aright. (3:98/103)

Elsewhere in the Qur'an the same idea is expressed by the word *awliya*, a word that reminds especially of the tribal bonds:

> And the men who believe and the women who believe are (*awliya*) protectors one of another. (9:72/71)

However, just as in the Old Testament, while maintaining all the fine obligations of hospitality and kindness toward those in need of them, the Qur'an is hard toward enemies. Muslim brotherhood is open to all those who wish to embrace Islam. But those who have not done so, or are not willing to do so, may not enjoy the civil or political rights that are reserved to Muslims alone. In this matter, there is no equality based on the sole rights of man as man. There is equality only after conversion. Other persons can claim at best only the status of guest or client.

> Muhammad is the messenger of God [Allah], and those who are with him are strong [*shadid*: violent, severe] against unbelievers, compassionate among themselves. (48:29)

Comparison between the Bible and the Qur'an on this particular point of brotherhood is not without danger. Not indeed from the theoretical standpoint, for the Incarnation has given to the neighbor a consistency that the idea did not have before: a Christian should love his neighbor with all his heart, whoever he may be. But in practice, to be fully just in such a comparison, one should not forget the parable of the mote and the beam.

15

The History of the Primitive Muslim Community

The verses that refer to the primitive Muslim community evidently belong to the peculiar Muslim patrimony. They are of no special or direct interest to us in this study of the Bible and the Qur'an. There are many such verses, and they present events as a sort of *gesta Dei per Musulmanos* (God's deeds through the Muslims). They must have had a special appeal to believers, as the narratives of battles appeal to groups of veterans who have taken part in them. To others, they are not of particular interest.

We should perhaps compare the very keen sense of God's presence in the biblical events of sacred history and the way in which Islam conceives God's role in its own primitive history. In the Qur'an, everything is traced back directly to God, as appears from the following verse, which recalls the affair of Badr in 624:

> It was not you who slew them; it was God who slew them.
> It was not you [Muhammad] who threw, it was God who threw, to test the believers graciously. Verily God hears and knows all things. (8:17)

Many texts refer to the "Holy War" (*Jihad*). One cannot extract from them a complete code of war policy. They are too fragmentary in character. When trying to get a coherent body of directions, the doctors of the Law added many personal views of their own.

In fact Muslim wars were conducted and considered as great adventures. Complex instincts (hunger, revenge, ambition, self-preservation) all contributed to their initiation. It was only afterward that motives were looked for to account for the undertaking. In any case it is certain that the Qur'an texts were not conducive to peace.

This question of the Muslim wars has caused extensive controversy. The countries that were invaded by Muslim armies and were not converted kept bitter memories of the events. The Muslims, on the contrary, have idealized them. Only after an examination of the facts—all of them, not only edifying episodes that are spotlighted—is one enabled to judge fairly.

Certainly from the beginning, Islam had an active warlike character. It acted in accordance with the laws of Bedouin warfare, even in one case against those very Bedouin laws. Muhammad, in person or through his lieutenants, led some twenty such expeditions against the Meccans, their allies, or other independent tribes. In the Qur'an, one hears the echoes of that martial activity. The Qur'anic texts have a variety of tones, but throughout we find a militant ideal that fed the eloquence of the preachers and fanned the zeal of the combatants for centuries.

When in the twentieth century the *Ahmadiyya* sect wanted to reinterpret the Qur'an by suppressing certain aspects of the Holy War, Muslims generally protested in the name of the Qur'an. Some verses state that it is necessary to fight in special cases:

> Fight in the way of Allah those who fight you; but be not transgressors; God does not love transgressors. (2:186/190)

The question, then, was to fight the Meccans who had refused to accept Islam and ill-treated the first believers. Such a fight, according to the law of the desert, was considered a normal counterstroke. Some modern Muslims interpret the text in a manner that extends beyond the first struggles of their fathers. They declare that, according to the Qur'an, only a defensive war would be legitimate, and they present the first Muslim conquests and the advance to Poitiers, even to China, as defensive campaigns. But the rest of the verse suggests something quite different:

And slay them wherever you find them [or, gain the mastery over them], and drive them out from where they have driven you out. The calamity [suffered by the believers] is more severe than the murder [of unbelievers]; but do not fight them by the Sacred Mosque before they fight you there. If they fight you, slay them. Such is the reward of the unbelievers. (2:187/191)

One of the texts especially promises the earth to the believers, in God's name, as an inheritance, and justifies in advance any attempt, peaceful or, within certain limits, warlike, for the purpose of attaining world hegemony:

God has promised to those of you who believe and do good deeds that He will make you heirs to the earth [or land], as He did for those before them. (24:54/55)

Some modern Muslims strive to minimize this text. One has only to read what the commentaries on the Qur'an say on this in order to see that most of them understand the text to mean really having rule and hegemony.

We hear it said at times that the Qur'an imposes conversion by force. Muslims reply that the Qur'an forbids the use of force in conversion. This problem should be defined accurately if we do not wish to engage in insoluble intricacies. What is meant by forced conversion? Is it one obtained by threatening with death those who are not converted? In this case, Muslims will reply that in Muhammad's time, their ancestors never killed pagans or people of the Book simply because such people refused conversion. The cases of forced conversions in the Middle Ages, such as those of young children captured in raids for slaves or janissaries, are regarded as illegal by many modern Muslim doctors of the Law and cannot be considered here.

Does this mean that Islam did not use force in its spreading? On the contrary. It is admitted that the Muslim armies have imposed by force a new order of things in the countries they conquered. The greatest part of the territories of the Muslim world was conquered by the force of arms. Only those were slain who resisted with weapons that implantation of the Pax Islamica. They were slain as enemies in war. Within the conquered lands, institutions were set up that through their actions helped gradual conversions to Islam and made almost impossible any reverse movement. Thus the power of the community has encouraged many conversions to Islam. At a time of massacres and condemnations, when an accused was in a tight corner, the non-Muslim could find an escape by becoming a Muslim. In Medina, during Muhammad's lifetime (as we have seen), the men of the Jewish tribe of the Qorayza were given a choice between conversion or death. Of some six hundred to nine hundred, only a very few individuals accepted Islam. It must be granted that for a long time a strong social pressure was exerted in Islam on non-Muslims. During the Middle Ages, some positions were denied them, but Islam left those who submitted to its hegemony free to organize themselves under a minority status considered inferior. The wish to escape from such a status, love for a Muslim woman whom only a Muslim may marry, and also the proselytisms of Muslim individuals have kept going the one-way system of conversion. As a rule, the reverse demands great force of character and exceptional circumstances within an Islamic country.

16

The Philosophy of the Religious History of the World

At the close of this all too brief study, we still have to situate the whole of the Qur'anic teaching in relation to the teaching of the Bible.

To the Muslim tradition everything is simple. The religious teaching of the Qur'an and that of the Bible must, a priori, be identical. If there are substantial differences, the Muslim only looks at the Qur'an. He disregards the biblical text, or at least he interprets it so as to make it agree with the Qur'an. This supposes an altogether casual attitude toward the biblical text. Hence, when one believes in the authenticity of the Bible, one cannot accept such an attitude.

Some Christians, in order to reduce the differences between the Bible and the Qur'an, rather tend to emphasize the originality of the Qur'an in relation to the Bible. They note the very vague character of the Qur'anic allusions to the essential teachings of the Bible. They insist on the Arab aspect of the Qur'an. They would look upon it as a witness to a purely Arab religious tradition, a sort of echo of a natural pre-Christian revelation connected with Abraham through Ishmael. According to their view, the Qur'an does

The translation here is based on the new text supplied by the author for this chapter.

not pass judgment on the "Christian fact". It rather belongs to a "psychological" time prior to Christ. Its anti-Christian portions affect only deviations that the Church herself condemns in the name of a very correct idea of the divine transcendence. It hardly needs to be said that this theologico-historical view of Islam deserves to be studied closely. If it were accepted, it would mean a complete revision of the Christian view of Islam. In any case, the noble-mindedness and the generosity of those who defend that thesis command our respect. However, to us personally, this view does not seem to be acceptable. First of all, because it goes against the whole Muslim tradition, which maintains that the Qur'an has passed judgment on the "Christian fact", and then because the rejection of a whole tradition on such an essential point would require other arguments in order to be accepted. That position does not take into account all that which archeology and epigraphy teach us about the pre-Islamic Arab religions. Absolute monotheism may exist in some Arab pre-Islamic currents; but such currents seem to be exceptional, and it is hard to say to what extent they do not depend on indirect biblical influences; but especially, the eschatological aspect of Islam, which is so important, does not appear at all in the pre-Islamic Arab religions. We know the scandal caused in Mecca by the preaching of those eschatological views. Mecca was totally unprepared for such eschatology. Moreover, the Qur'an, as we have tried to show, means clearly to bring the final word, the last revelation. It means clearly to pass judgment on the "Christian fact", or at least on the nondivinity of Christ. It does so, realizing fully the implications of its statements, even if it does not go into theological details about the matter. It was not necessary to be a theologian in order to know that some saw in Christ more than a creature, while others refused to see in Him anything more than a man, a new Adam, whom God had favored in a special manner. There is in the Qur'an a very Arabic affectivity; but there are also in it many extrabiblical elements. A last indication of the importance of the biblical traditions in Islam is to be found in the Arabs' proper names. Before Islam, purely biblical names do not occur. But after the rise of Islam those names become frequent, at least current. Their introduction cannot be explained as due to a purely Arab tradition, but rather as due to the biblical aspect of the Qur'an.

The question could be asked whether the current follows a chronological rule in the selection the Qur'an makes among the biblical elements; or, to put it in another way, if the biblical elements of the Qur'an correspond to a particular stage of the biblical revelation. It is a fact that the Qur'anic narratives concerning Abraham and especially Moses are fuller than the others. However, the question of this relative importance should not deceive us. The Qur'an has elements corresponding to all stages of the biblical revelation: accounts related to those of the Pentateuch; also in the various chapters we encounter verses on monotheism and creation, which remind us of some texts of Isaiah. The struggle against idolatry that appears on almost every page of the Qur'an is the leitmotiv of the prophetic oracles of the Bible; the eschatology reminds us of the whole apocalyptic literature that is of late date. The frequent mention of the Torah in the Qur'an could represent a religious stage comparable to that of the Pentateuch. Personally, we had thought so some years ago. But it does not seem to us now that this view can be defended. The Qur'an contains elements revealed in the Bible at different dates. It takes its stand on the fundamental problem of Christianity when it rejects the divinity of Christ! Its position, thus, is close to that of rabbinic Judaism. However, its tendencies are Christianizing. There is in the Qur'an more than mere respect for the person of Jesus. Who in Jewish orthodox circles would have dared to call Jesus "Word of God" and "Messiah", when one realizes the full implications of such titles?

Yet, there is in the Bible a whole religious aspect that has no equivalent in the Qur'an, the historical aspect properly so-called, that of the progressive revelation of God's love for His people, through all the vicissitudes of history; with the growing awareness of the grievous character of sin considered as an offense against God's love and the needs of all mankind, that of "the poor of Yahweh". In fact, in the Qur'an, the history of Israel is limited to the history of Moses and his ancestors; in short, the nomadic period of the Hebrews.

Such a state of things may escape us at first sight, because the Qur'an mentions a number of later personages; but it gives them only anecdotic notice; so for Saul and Goliath; it recalls briefly Elijah's fight against the Baals, a brief allusion to Job and Jonah and the prophets slain by the Jews. Of the great prophets such as Isaiah, Jeremiah, and Ezekiel, some surahs have preserved something of the ardor of the fight against idolatry and of the emphasis on the worship of the One God, Creator of all things. But the Qur'an ignores the lesson of the Exile on the seriousness of sin. There is at best an allusion to the fact of the Exile (17:5–7). A little more space is devoted to David and Solomon. David is credited with the Psalms. Solomon's power over the jinns is mentioned, but the account is something quite outside the biblical data (34:10–12).

Though the Qur'an refers frequently to the Torah given to Moses, in fact only some elements of it are kept by the Qur'an; the Muslims criticize the Pentateuch somewhat like the Ebionites of the Pseudo-Clementines.

When the Qur'an speaks of the Torah given to Moses, the term must be taken in the strict sense of the Pentateuch; the word itself, Torah in Hebrew, is first used for the five books of the Pentateuch. As the Bible is presented in fact in the Qur'an, it comprises only the Pentateuch and the Gospel (in the singular), and as far as the Pentateuch is concerned, it means not the whole text, but only selected portions. Some texts from the beginning of the Bible, especially those characteristic of the anthropomorphic style, find no place in the Qur'an, which is more strict, more intransigent in its manner of speaking of God.

From this there flows a very serious consequence. The religious view of the history of the world in the Qur'an differs completely from that of orthodox Judaism and of Christianity. On this capital point, at least for the first part of the history of Israel until the Messiah, Jews and Christians hold the same positions.

The Qur'an and the Pentateuch agree in teaching that God made a covenant with the Israelites on Sinai. But what kind of covenant? That is the question.

The Pentateuch is not the whole Bible, and some matters to which it refers will be elucidated in the sequel of the sacred history and in the revelations of the prophets. Thus on what point is the covenant firm? In the oracles, God uses very strong terms. The infidelities of the Jews are described under the figure of adultery. But God does not abandon the Children of Israel. They represent His people, whom He chastises when they sin. Nevertheless it is through them that the salvation of the world is to be accomplished. This idea is one of the leitmotivs of the Bible; it cannot have been introduced through falsifications or forgeries of texts, for the very structure of history cannot be falsified.

Together with this role given to the Jewish people in the salvation of the world, a role that Christianity cannot deny without losing its very substance, the Bible speaks of the expectation of the Messiah. The promise was made to David; the royal house of David is to subsist forever (cf. 2 Sam 7). The Messiah (a Semitic word meaning "Anointed"—"Christ", in Greek; the one who has received the royal unction) is to fulfill that promise in a manner that could not be suspected at first. The text of Samuel represents, as noted in the Jerusalem Bible, "the first link in the prophecies concerning 'the Messiah, son of David' ". The other links are known. When the Davidic dynasty seemed on the point of disappearing, prophets recalled that the promise was still valid. Then there were anxious moments when the political situation of the Babylonian Captivity or the difficult years that followed seemed to show that the fulfillment receded more and more. The faith in the coming Messiah encouraged by the prophets did not vanish. Daniel kept the hope alive. In the years that preceded Jesus, the expectation was more and more living.

In the Old Testament, all the religious history is centered on that promise, the call of the people of God. In the New Testament, the coming of the Messiah, the incarnate Word, born from David according to the flesh, represents for the Christian the high point of mankind's history, with the revelation of the fact that God is love, the supernatural adoption of the believers through grace alone, the founding of the Church against which nothing shall prevail, the great commandment of charity, the outpouring of the Holy Spirit in the souls. The kingdom of God is here already in the form it must have on earth, with struggles and suffering at times. After such gifts, revelation is closed. The question now is to preach the good news of the Gospel, to announce it to all nations; and each one, while doing his duty in his place, waits for the Day of Judgment, when the Son of Man shall come back on the clouds to judge the living and the dead. And His reign shall have no end. What a long way this is from the first call to Abraham!

For Islam, on the contrary, there is no progress in the revelation of the mystery of God. The prophets periodically remind men of the religion, an unchangeable natural religion. The various communities they visit are without any bond among them, a mere juxtaposition in time. The great Qur'anic Law of history, that unchangeable custom of God in His dealing with man, is that the people rebellious against God's messengers are destroyed (Noah and the Flood, the prophets of Arabia, Lot and the destruction of his city, Moses and the Red Sea swallowing up Pharaoh's army). They were then replaced by others who took their succession. That Law has not been applied for a long time. But Islam teaches still that the infidelity of peoples is punished here below. For God, as the Qur'an says, has pledged Himself to give victory to the believers. Thus it is that Islam presents itself as the last historical community in the history of the world, destined now to intransigent monotheism, destined to call upon men to worship their Creator like the shadow that lengthens at the end of the day.

> Do they seek for another religion than that of God while those who are in heaven and earth submit to Him willingly or unwillingly and shall return to Him? (3:77/83)

This is the spirit in which Islam has struggled and struggles to obey the summons of the Qur'an. Five times a day the Muezzins proclaim to the world the unity of God and their faith in Muhammad's vision. Of old the Muslim conquerors supported the preaching of Islam. Merchants spread their faith as they traveled. All that is good in the natural virtues, in human affections, generosity, is seen by the Muslims in the light of the Qur'an. Politics and religion united to spread a new order of things.

CONCLUSION

Two worlds exist now. It was necessary to call attention to the differences in order to prevent any misunderstanding. The reader will have noted them as we went along. However, in conclusion, let us look at what we have in common. Let us not forget, first of all, that Muslims and Christians are men. All of us are sons of Adam. There are essentially human values that we find wherever men know how to respond to what is best in them. Both the Qur'an and the Bible evoke a number of these values—love of parents, sacrifice, self-devotion, kindness, and many others.

When they are mentioned in connection with particular incidents, for instance, forgiveness to those who had slandered Ayesha, the Qur'anic text rises from a particular case to a more general level. After inviting the hearers to mutual forgiveness, the Qur'an adds:

> Do you not wish that God should forgive you? God is most forgiving and merciful. (24:22)

There is here an appeal to something higher, which will perhaps help to explain how in the Gospel forgiving our brethren is the *conditio sine qua non* of divine forgiveness. So also in the case of almsgiving. The Qur'an on occasion praises the one who hides his generosity:

> If you give alms publicly, it is well; and if you conceal them and give them to those in need, it is better for you and it will efface some of your evil deeds. (2:273/271)

97

Here again we have something that urges one to higher perfection and enables him to pass on to the teaching of the Sermon on the Mount, with its appeals to generous souls.

Sometimes, great tactfulness will be needed. When speaking of God, the Bible uses some expressions that are not found in the Qur'an and that are puzzling to Muslims. Thus comparisons based on human psychology and meant to convey an idea of God's love for His people, likened to a man's love for his wife, and so forth. This is not the Qur'an's way of expressing things. No doubt it will be possible to make our attitude understood by appealing to man's experience, to an inborn sense of the values intended in such expressions, by emphasizing that such ways of speaking do not imply any disrespect for divine transcendence. A young Muslim father, proud of the birth of his firstborn son, will understand, if the matter is handled delicately, why the Bible applies to God the concept of paternal love. An example illustrates the thought quite well. It is a passage in a modern commentary on the Qur'an. The author wrote it some thirty years ago. He spoke of a father's love for his son in connection with a piece of news that was being talked about around him. In spite of the unworthy conduct of the son, on hearing of his illness, the Sheikh hastened to his son's bedside, forgetting the wrong he had done. The writer used this fact to make people understand the idea of God's love. Thus, without being aware of it, he was voicing the spirit of the parable of the Prodigal Son.

The Qur'an insists on the idea that man's sin does not harm God, but only hurts the sinner himself. It will be more difficult to explain the notion of sin as an offense to God, of the duty of expiation, and so forth. But man has a sense of honor, and when he realizes all that which the hatred of atheists destroys in the hearts of men, he can start from this to rise to the honor of God on this earth, and the injury to God caused by sin. The Pseudo-Gospel of Barnabas, an apocryphon from the Middle Ages that has found readers among Muslims during the last fifty years, presents the matter in that manner: sin as an insult to God's honor, and Muslims understand. We can find such starting points to carry across Christian ideas.

Christians and Muslims thus share those human values to which one can appeal to help mutual understanding. They find in themselves the same will to respect the immense greatness of God, of the Lord God who must be served first. "The Lord God is to be served first" might be our common motto.

If we firmly believe that man has been called by Christ to graces of illimitable measure—of intimate life with God—we must never forget that those graces never should make us lose, in any way, our absolute respect for God's greatness. On the contrary, they should help us to become more conscious of our own unworthiness and of our poverty in the presence of the mystery of the purity, holiness, goodness, and power of the Living God. Everything we have is His gift. After hearing Jesus' word to the Samaritan woman: "If you knew the gift of God" (Jn 4:10), the Christian can only bow in adoration, full of love and humility, and sing with the utmost respect: "God Alone is Great." Thus he uses the words used by his brethren, though for him the mystery of that Greatness includes much more: the mystery of God's infinite love in Himself.

APPENDIX ONE

NOSTRA AETATE, DECLARATION
ON THE RELATION OF THE CHURCH
TO NON-CHRISTIAN RELIGIONS

Vatican II, October 28, 1965

1. In this age of ours, when men are drawing more closely together and the bonds of friendship between different peoples are being strengthened, the Church examines with greater care the relation which she has to non-Christian religions. Ever aware of her duty to foster unity and charity among individuals, and even among nations, she reflects at the outset on what men have in common and what tends to promote fellowship among them.

All men form but one community. This is so because all stem from the one stock which God created to people the entire earth (cf. Acts 17:26), and also because all share a common destiny, namely God. His providence, evident goodness, and saving designs extend to all men (cf. Wis. 8:1; Acts 14:17; Rom. 2:6–7; 1 Tim. 2:4) against the day when the

Translated by Father Killian, O.C.S.O., in *Vatican Council II: The Conciliar and Post Conciliar Documents*, ed. Austin Flannery, new rev. ed. (Northport, N.Y.: Costello Publishing, 1992, pp. 738–42). Used by permission.

elect are gathered together in the holy city which is illu-
mined by the glory of God, and in whose splendor all peoples will walk (cf. Apoc. 21:23 ff.).

Men look to their different religions for an answer to the
unsolved riddles of human existence. The problems that weigh
heavily on the hearts of men are the same today as in the
ages past. What is man? What is the meaning and purpose of
life? What is upright behavior, and what is sinful? Where
does suffering originate, and what end does it serve? How
can genuine happiness be found? What happens at death?
What is judgment? What reward follows death? And finally,
what is the ultimate mystery, beyond human explanation,
which embraces our entire existence, from which we take
our origin and towards which we tend?

2. Throughout history even to the present day, there is
found among different peoples a certain awareness of a hidden power, which lies behind the course of nature and the
events of human life. At times there is present even a recognition of a supreme being, or still more of a Father. This
awareness and recognition results in a way of life that is im-
bued with a deep religious sense. The religions which are
found in more advanced civilizations endeavor by way of
well-defined concepts and exact language to answer these
questions. . . . Religions which are found throughout the
world attempt in their own ways to calm the hearts of men
by outlining a program of life covering doctrine, moral precepts and sacred rites.

The Catholic Church rejects nothing of what is true and holy
in these religions. She has a high regard for the manner of life
and conduct, the precepts and doctrines which, although dif-
fering in many ways from her own teaching, nevertheless often reflect a ray of that truth which enlightens all men. Yet she

proclaims and is in duty bound to proclaim without fail, Christ who is the way, the truth and the life (Jn. 1:6). In him, in whom God reconciled all things to himself (2 Cor. 5:18–19), men find the fulness of their religious life.

The Church, therefore, urges her sons to enter with prudence and charity into discussions and collaboration with members of other religions. Let Christians, while witnessing to their own faith and way of life, acknowledge, preserve and encourage the spiritual and moral truths found among non-Christians, also their social life and culture.

3. The Church has also a high regard for the Muslims. They worship God, who is one, living and subsistent, merciful and almighty, the Creator of heaven and earth,[1] who has also spoken to men. They strive to submit themselves without reserve to the hidden decrees of God, just as Abraham submitted himself to God's plan, to whose faith Muslims eagerly link their own. Although not acknowledging him as God, they venerate Jesus as a prophet, his virgin Mother they also honor, and even at times devoutly invoke. Further, they await the day of judgment and the reward of God following the resurrection of the dead. For this reason they highly esteem an upright life and worship God, especially by way of prayer, alms-deeds and fasting.

Over the centuries many quarrels and dissensions have arisen between Christians and Muslims. The sacred Council now pleads with all to forget the past, and urges that a sincere effort be made to achieve mutual understanding; for the benefit of all men, let them together preserve and promote peace, liberty, social justice and moral values. . . .

[1] Cf. St. Gregory VII, Letter 21 to Anzir (Nacir), King of Mauretania (*PL* 148, cols. 450ff.).

5. We cannot truly pray to God the Father of all if we treat any people in other than brotherly fashion, for all men are created in God's image. Man's relation to God the Father and man's relation to his fellow-men are so dependent on each other that the Scripture says "he who does not love, does not know God" (1 Jn. 4:8).

There is no basis therefore, either in theory or in practice for any discrimination between individual and individual, or between people and people arising either from human dignity or from the rights which flow from it.

Therefore, the Church reproves, as foreign to the mind of Christ, any discrimination against people or any harassment of them on the basis of their race, color, condition in life or religion. Accordingly, following the footsteps of the holy apostles Peter and Paul, the sacred Council earnestly begs the Christian faithful to "conduct themselves well among the Gentiles" (1 Pet. 2:12) and if possible, as far as depends on them, to be at peace with all men (cf. Rom. 12:18) and in that way to be true sons of the Father who is in heaven (cf. Mt. 5:45).

APPENDIX TWO

DIALOGUE WITH MUSLIMS FROM THE POINT OF VIEW OF THE CATHOLIC CHURCH: BASES, AIMS, EXPERIENCES

by Francis Cardinal Arinze

Introduction

The concept of dialogue was not a marginal issue to the Fathers of the Second Vatican Council (1962–65). In addition to ecumenical dialogue (i.e., dialogue with other Christians), which is consistently stressed in the Council documents, the need for dialogue with people of other religions is a recurring theme in the Council documents.

Basic Common Beliefs

In their basic beliefs, Christians and Muslims have much in common. They believe in God Who is one, Creator, provider, merciful, all-powerful and final judge of all human beings. Jews,

Excerpts from Lecture given in Munich at the celebration of the tenth anniversary of the "Ökumenische Kontaktstelle für Nichtchristen in der Erzdiözese München und Freising" (Ecumenical association for non-Christians in the Archdiocese of Munich and Freising), 13 April 1989. Published as Chapter 22 in Francis Cardinal Arinze, *The Church in Dialogue: Walking with Other Religions* (San Francisco: Ignatius Press, 1990), pp. 313–29.

Christians and Muslims somehow trace their faith back to Abraham. Christians and Muslims believe that details of their daily lives should be governed by obedience to God's will and that prayer, fasting and almsgiving are necessary.

The reverence and love which Muslims have for Jesus and the honour which they give to His Virgin Mother Mary are a bond which Christians have with no other religious group. Christians can be surprised to learn that Mary is mentioned nineteen times in the Bible but thirty-four times in the Qur'an, where she is called "the greatest of all women". Moreover, Mary is the only woman mentioned by name in the Qur'an. A saying of Muhammad preserved by Muslims relates: "Every person born into this world has been touched by sin, except Jesus and his mother."

Just as these common elements of belief make the Islamic community one which is close to Christians in faith, so the Qur'an holds that "and you will find that the nearest of those in friendship to those who believe [Muslims] are they who say, 'We are Christians'; that is because they have priests and monks, and they are not arrogant" (Qur'an 5:85).

Profound Differences

There should be no misunderstanding. The existence of these genuine elements which we share with Muslims does not mean that there are not real and even profound differences between the two religions. Muslims honour Jesus as one of the greatest prophets and the "Seal of Holiness", but, unlike Christians, they do not accept Him as "more than a prophet", that unique relationship to the Father which leads Christians to acknowledge and adore Jesus as "Son of God". Consequently, Christians honour the Blessed Virgin Mary as Mother of God. Muslims do not accept this. Still more fundamental is the Christian faith in the Most Blessed Trinity, the mystery of Three Persons in one God, Father, Son and Holy Spirit, which is not accepted by Muslims, who stress God's absolute Unity.

Other differences, perhaps more subtle yet nevertheless basic to our self-understanding as people of faith, can also be found. For Christians, the Jewish law was fulfilled and completed in the person of Jesus, Who left us, by word and example, the law of love. We believe that this new and eternal covenant of God's love was accomplished by Jesus' death on the Cross and God's raising Him to new life.

This drama of salvation, of God entering personally into human history to save us, is absent in Islam. According to Islam, Jesus did not die on the Cross but was miraculously raised into heaven, where He awaits His final return to earth before the Last Day. According to Islam, God's message has not been incarnated in a man, Jesus Christ, but rather delivered in a book, in the Qur'an. This book gives guidance to Muslims to follow the path of obedience to God's law, which, they believe, leads to salvation. For Christians, public revelation is full, complete and concluded in Jesus Christ. And because the Incarnation and Redemption are denied in Islam, the whole idea of salvation is different in this religion.

Right to Religious Freedom

The Catholic Church does not ignore the differences between her beliefs and those of Muslims, and indeed of other believers. But the Church maintains that the human person has fundamental right to freedom of religion.

> This freedom means that all men are to be immune from coercion on the part of individuals or of social groups and of

any human power, in such wise that in matters religious no one is to be forced to act in a manner contrary to his own beliefs. Nor is anyone to be restrained from acting in accordance with his own beliefs, whether privately or publicly, whether alone or in association with others, within due limits (DH, no. 2).

The basic God-given endowment of intellect and free will which all human beings have is a basis for dialogue, more so in matters religious.

Experience in Three Shrines of Our Lady

I might also mention the shrine of Our Lady's House in Ephesus, where, according to ancient tradition, she lived with Saint John after Jesus' ascension. This shrine has become better known among European Christians through the writings of the nineteenth-century German mystic Catherine Emmerich, although for centuries it has been a place of pilgrimage for Christians and Muslims in Turkey. This past year, more than two hundred thousand visitors came to this simple two-room house on an isolated mountaintop outside the ancient city. There are two Capuchin monks, both fluent in Arabic and Turkish, to meet the guests and be present for religious discussions. The monks estimate that about half their visitors are Muslims and half Christians.

Muslims visit the beautiful Basilica of Our Lady of Africa at the seaside in Algiers and pray there. The artistic baldacchino in which the statue of Our Lady of Africa rests in this basilica was designed by a Muslim as his gift to the shrine.

In the village of Medroussa near Tiaret, in Algeria, Spanish Catholics had long ago built a shrine to the Virgin Mary. When most of the Europeans left the country in the early 1960s, the local Muslims continued to maintain the shrine and went there to pray. Recently, they have called the attention of the local bishop to the availability of the shrine.

Good Understanding between Individual Muslims and Christians

Good Muslims revere holy persons, even when they are Christian. In this they are following the precepts of the Qur'an, which speaks highly of Christian monks. The Algerian sheikh of a Sufi order in Paris published a letter stating he would like to meet Mother Teresa; since she was a holy woman, they would have much to talk about. It is known that in the days of the former President of Pakistan, each time Mother Teresa arrived in that country, the President's private plane would be waiting at the airport to take her first to meet the President, after which she would be free to go about her business.

A priest who was living alone in a small house in a working-class neighborhood in a Middle Eastern city recently related that when it became known among the inhabitants of the 100 percent Muslim district that there was a monk living among them, people would come regularly to bring him hot meals, deliver his mail, even do his laundry and clean the house. He claims that in two years, he was never treated with anything but warmth and respect.

In the city of Peshawar, in the predominantly Afghan region of Pakistan's frontier province, an elderly Irish missionary sister who had been teaching in a girls' school for several decades became seriously ill. When it became known in the city that the sister was in the hospital, the mayor ordered offices and shops in the city closed for an hour so that all could pray for the recovery of the sister.

In October last year during a visit to Pakistan, I was happy to call on a distinguished Muslim of the Sufi order, Mr. Barkat

Ali, who lives near Faisalabad. He lives a life of prayer and devotion to his fellowman. He has no bank account. He keeps no money overnight. He receives considerable sums of money and distributes all of it to the poor the same day. He wore no sandals and lived in a very poor shelter. He is very dedicated to the Qur'an. He spoke words of wisdom and love. I praised God for endowing this man with so much goodness.

Conclusion

Neither the Vatican Council nor the recent Popes have ever claimed that dialogue is easy. It is not. Moreover, Christians and Muslims are only at the beginning stages of this new emphasis on relationships. Many centuries of conflict, mis-understanding and mutual suspicion are difficult to over-come in a short time. The Holy Father in Assisi in 1986 stressed that peace cannot come solely from human efforts but is simultaneously a gift from God, a gift for which we must constantly ask in humble prayer. In the same way a deep attitude of respectful fraternity and esteem between Christians and Muslims can come about, not solely from our human efforts at dialogue but above all from God's grace. Even as we strive to multiply the occasions of dialogue at all levels, we must also pray often for the divine gift of harmo-nious and mutually enriching relations between Christians and Muslims throughout the world.

APPENDIX THREE

"Muslim and Christian Communities Should Be in Respectful Dialogue"

by John Paul II

On Sunday evening at 6:15 p.m., 6 May, the Holy Father left the Syrian Orthodox Cathedral to go to the Umayyad Great Mosque of Damascus, to visit the memorial of St. John the Baptist with the Grand Mufti, Sheik Ahmad Kuftaro, and other Muslim authorities. In the courtyard of the mosque the Holy Father met with the Muslim authorities and gave the following address in English. "The fact that we are meeting in this renowned place of prayer reminds us that man is a spiritual being, called to acknowledge the absolute priority of God in all things."

Dear Muslim Friends,
As-salámū 'aláikum!

1. I give heartfelt praise to Almighty God for the grace of this meeting. I am most grateful for your warm welcome, in the tradition of hospitality so cherished by the people of this region. I thank especially the Minister of the Waqf and the Grand Mufti for their gracious greetings, which put into words the great yearning for peace which fills the hearts of all people

Published in *L'Osservatore romano*, May 9, 2001, pp. 10–11.

of good will. My Jubilee Pilgrimage has been marked by important meetings with Muslim leaders in Cairo and Jerusalem, and now I am deeply moved to be your guest here in the great Umayyad Mosque, so rich in religious history. Your land is dear to Christians: here our religion has known vital moments of its growth and doctrinal development, and here are found Christian communities which have lived in peace and harmony with their Muslim neighbours for many centuries.

John the Baptist, example of search for truth and justice

2. We are meeting close to what both Christians and Muslims regard as the tomb of John the Baptist, known as *Yahya* in the Muslim tradition. The son of Zechariah is a figure of prime importance in the history of Christianity, for he was the Precursor who prepared the way for Christ. John's life, wholly dedicated to God, was crowned by martyrdom. May his witness enlighten all who venerate his memory here, so that they—and we too—may understand that life's great task is to seek God's truth and justice.

The fact that we are meeting in this renowned place of prayer reminds us that man is a spiritual being, called to acknowledge and respect the absolute priority of God in all things. Christians and Muslims agree that the encounter with God in prayer is the necessary nourishment of our souls, without which our hearts wither and our will no longer strives for good but succumbs to evil.

Religious leaders should present communities as being in dialogue, not in conflict

3. Both Muslims and Christians prize their places of prayer, as oases where they meet the All Merciful God on the jour-

ney to eternal life, and where they meet their brothers and sisters in the bond of religion. When, on the occasion of weddings or funerals or other celebrations, Christians and Muslims remain in silent respect at the other's prayer, they bear witness to what unites them without disguising or denying the things that separate.

It is in mosques and churches that the Muslim and Christian communities shape their religious identity, and it is there that the young receive a significant part of their religious education. What sense of identity is instilled in young Christians and young Muslims in our churches and mosques? It is my ardent hope that Muslim and Christian religious leaders and teachers will present our two great religious communities *as communities in respectful dialogue, never more as communities in conflict*. It is crucial for the young to be taught the ways of respect and understanding, so that they will not be led to misuse religion itself to promote or justify hatred and violence. Violence destroys the image of the Creator in his creatures, and should never be considered as the fruit of religious conviction.

Interreligious dialogue leads to partnership for the good of the human family

4. I truly hope that our meeting today in the Umayyad Mosque will signal our determination to advance interreligious dialogue between the Catholic Church and Islam. This dialogue has gained momentum in recent decades; and today we can be grateful for the road we have travelled together so far. At the highest level, the Pontifical Council for Interreligious Dialogue represents the Catholic Church in this task. For more than 30 years the Council has sent a message to Muslims on the occasion of *Íd al-Fitr* at the close of Ramadan, and I am very happy that this gesture has been

welcomed by many Muslims as a sign of growing friendship between us. In recent years the Council has established a liaison committee with international Islamic Organizations, and also with *al-Azhar* in Egypt, which I had the pleasure of visiting last year.

It is important that Muslims and Christians continue to explore philosophical and theological questions together, in order to come to a more objective and comprehensive knowledge of each other's religious beliefs. Better mutual understanding will surely lead, at the practical level, to a new way of presenting our two religions *not in opposition*, as has happened too often in the past, *but in partnership for the good of the human family*.

Interreligious dialogue is most effective when it springs from the experience of "living with each other" from day to day within the same community and culture. In Syria, Christians and Muslims have lived side by side for centuries, and a rich dialogue of life has gone on unceasingly. Every individual and every family knows moments of harmony, and other moments when dialogue has broken down. The positive experiences must strengthen our communities in the hope of peace; and the negative experiences should not be allowed to undermine that hope. For all the times that Muslims and Christians have offended one another, we need to seek forgiveness from the Almighty and to offer each other forgiveness. Jesus teaches us that we must pardon others' offences if God is to pardon us our sins (cf. Mt 6:14).

As members of the one human family and as believers, we have obligations to the common good, to justice and to solidarity. Interreligious dialogue will lead to many forms of cooperation, especially in responding to the duty to care for the poor and the weak. These are the signs that our worship of God is genuine.

5. As we make our way through life towards our heavenly destiny, Christians feel the company of Mary, the Mother of Jesus; and Islam too pays tribute to Mary and hails her as "chosen above the women of the world" (*Quran*, III:42). The Virgin of Nazareth, the Lady of *Saydnâya*, has taught us that God protects the humble and "scatters the proud in the imagination of the hearts" (Lk 1:51). May the hearts of Christians and Muslims turn to one another with feelings of brotherhood and friendship, so that the Almighty may bless us with the peace which heaven alone can give. To the One, Merciful God be praise and glory for ever. Amen.

APPENDIX FOUR

"Genuine Peace Is a Gift from God; I Raise My Heart and Voice with Great Intensity"

by John Paul II

On Monday morning, 7 May, after visiting the places of the Apostle Paul, the Holy Father traveled to Qunaytra, where in the Greek Orthodox Church in Qunaytra, at the Golan Heights, he offered the following prayer for peace in English.

"*Blessed are the peacemakers, for they shall be called sons of God*" (Mt 5:9). From this place, so disfigured by war, I wish to raise my heart and voice in prayer for peace in the Holy Land and in the whole world. Genuine peace is a gift from God. Our openness to that gift requires a conversion of heart and a conscience obedient to his Law. Mindful of the sad news of the conflicts and deaths which even today arrives from Gaza, my prayer becomes more intense.

God of infinite mercy and goodness,
with grateful hearts we pray to you today
in this land where St Paul once walked.

Published in *L'Osservatore romano*, May 9, 2001, p. 11.

To the nations he proclaimed
the truth that God was in Christ
reconciling the world to himself (cf. 2 Cor 5:19).

May your voice resound in the hearts
of all men and women,
as you call them to follow the path
of reconciliation and peace,
and to be merciful as you are merciful.

Lord, you speak words of peace to your people
and to all who turn to you in their hearts (cf. Ps 85:9).

We pray to you for the peoples of the Middle East.

Help them to break down the walls of hostility and division
and to build together a world of justice and solidarity.
Lord, you create new heavens and a new earth
(cf. Is 65:17).

To you we entrust the young people of these lands.

In their hearts they aspire to a brighter future;
strengthen their resolve to be men and women of peace,
and heralds of new hope to their peoples.

Father, you make justice spring forth from the earth (cf. Is 45:8).

We pray for the civil leaders of this region
that they may strive to satisfy
their peoples' rightful aspirations,
and educate the young in the ways of justice and good.

Inspire them to work generously for the common good,
to respect the inalienable dignity of every person
and the fundamental rights which have their origin
in the image and likeness of the Creator
impressed upon each and every human being.

In a special way we pray for the leaders
of this noble land of Syria.

Grant them wisdom, farsightedness and perseverance;
may they never yield to discouragement
in their challenging task
of building the lasting peace for which their people yearn.

Heavenly Father,
in this place which saw the conversion of the Apostle Paul,
we pray for all who believe in the Gospel of Jesus Christ.

Guide their steps in truth and love.

May they be one as you are one, with the Son and the
Holy Spirit.

May they bear witness to the peace
which surpasses all understanding (cf. Phil 4:7)
and to the light which triumphs over the darkness
of hostility, sin and death.
Lord of heaven and earth, Creator
of the one human family,
we pray for the followers of all religions.

May they seek your will in prayer and purity of heart;
may they adore you and worship your holy name.

Lead them to find in you the strength
to overcome fear and distrust,
to grow in friendship and to live together in harmony.

Merciful Father,
may all believers find the courage to forgive one another,
so that the wounds of the past may be healed,
and not be a pretext for further suffering in the present.

May this happen above all in the Holy Land,
this land which you have blessed with so many signs

of your Providence,
and where you have revealed yourself as the God of Love.

To the Mother of Jesus, the ever blessed Virgin Mary,
we entrust the men and women living in the land
where Jesus once lived.

Following her example, may they listen
to the word of God,
and have respect and compassion for others,
especially those who differ from them.

May they be inspired to oneness of heart and mind,
in working for a world that will be a true home
for all its peoples!

Salam! Salam! Salam!

Amen!

APPENDIX FIVE

MARY AND THE MOSLEMS

by Fulton J. Sheen

Islam is the only great post-Christian religion of the world.
Because it had its origin in the seventh century under Mohammed, it was possible to unite within it some elements of
Christianity and of Judaism, along with particular customs
of Arabia. Islam takes the doctrine of the unity of God, His
Majesty and His Creative Power, and uses it, in part, as a
basis for the repudiation of Christ, the Son of God. Misunderstanding the notion of the Trinity, Mohammed made
Christ a prophet announcing *him*, just as, to Christians, Isa-
ias and John the Baptist are prophets announcing Christ.

The Christian European West barely escaped destruction
at the hands of the Moslems. At one point they were stopped
near Tours, and at another point, later on in time, outside
the gates of Vienna. The Church throughout northern Africa was practically destroyed by Moslem power, and at the
present hour the Moslems are beginning to rise again.

This chapter is reprinted from *The World's First Love*, © 1952 by Fulton J.
Sheen, published by McGraw-Hill Book Company, Inc., New York. Re-
printed with permission of The Society for the Propagation of the Faith, New
York, N.Y.

If Islam is a heresy, as Hilaire Belloc believes it to be, it is the only heresy that has never declined. Others have had a moment of vigor, then gone into doctrinal decay at the death of the leader, and finally evaporated in a vague social movement. Islam, on the contrary, has only had its first phase. There was never a time in which it declined, either in numbers or in the devotion of its followers.

The missionary effort of the Church toward this group has been, at least on the surface, a failure, for the Moslems are so far almost unconvertible. The reason is that for a follower of Mohammed to become a Christian is much like a Christian becoming a Jew. The Moslems believe that they have the final and definitive revelation of God to the world and that Christ was only a prophet announcing Mohammed, the last of God's real prophets.

At the present time, the hatred of the Moslem countries against the West is becoming a hatred against Christianity itself. Although the statesmen have not yet taken it into account, there is still grave danger that the temporal power of Islam may return and, with it, the menace that it may shake off a West that has ceased to be Christian and affirm itself as a great anti-Christian world power. Moslem writers say, "When the locust swarms darken vast countries, they bear on their wings these Arabic words: 'We are God's host, each of us has ninety-nine eggs, and if we had a hundred, we should lay waste the world with all that is in it.' "

The problem is, How shall we prevent the hatching of the hundredth egg? It is our firm belief that the fears some entertain concerning the Moslems are not to be realized, but that Islam, instead, will eventually be converted to Christianity—and in a way that even some of our missionaries never suspect. It is our belief that this will happen not through the direct teaching of Christianity but through a summoning of the Moslems to a veneration of the Mother of God. This is the line of argument:

The Koran, which is the Bible of the Moslems, has many passages concerning the Blessed Virgin. First of all, the Koran believes in her Immaculate Conception and also in her Virgin Birth. The third chapter of the Koran places the history of Mary's family in a genealogy that goes back through Abraham, Noah, and Adam. When one compares the Koran's description of the birth of Mary with the apocryphal gospel of the birth of Mary, one is tempted to believe that Mohammed very much depended upon the latter. Both books describe the old age and the definite sterility of the mother of Mary. When, however, she conceives, the mother of Mary is made to say in the Koran: "O Lord, I vow and I consecrate to you what is already within me. Accept it from me."

When Mary is born, the mother says: "And I consecrate her with all of her posterity under thy protection, O Lord, against Satan!"

The Koran passes over Joseph in the life of Mary, but the Moslem tradition knows his name and has some familiarity with him. In this tradition, Joseph is made to speak to Mary, who is a virgin. As he inquired how she conceived Jesus without a father, Mary answered: "Do you not know that God, when He created the wheat, had no need of seed, and that God by His power made the trees grow without the help of rain? All that God had to do was to say, 'So be it', and it was done."

The Koran has also verses on the Annunciation, Visitation, and Nativity. Angels are pictured as accompanying the Blessed Mother and saying: "Oh, Mary, God has chosen you and purified you, and elected you above all the women of the earth." In the nineteenth chapter of the Koran there are forty-one verses on Jesus and Mary. There is such a strong defense of the virginity of Mary here that the Koran, in the fourth book, attributes the condemnation of the Jews to their monstrous calumny against the Virgin Mary.

Mary, then, is for the Moslems the true *Sayyida*, or Lady. The only possible serious rival to her in their creed would be Fatima, the daughter of Mohammed himself. But after the death of Fatima, Mohammed wrote: "Thou shalt be the most blessed of all the women in Paradise, after Mary." In a variant of the text, Fatima is made to say: "I surpass all the women, except Mary."

This brings us to our second point, namely, why the Blessed Mother, in this twentieth century, should have revealed herself in the insignificant little village of Fatima, so that to all future generations she would be known as Our Lady of Fatima. Since nothing ever happens out of Heaven except with a finesse of all details, I believe that the Blessed Virgin chose to be known as "Our Lady of Fatima" as a pledge and a sign of hope to the Moslem people and as an assurance that they, who show her so much respect, will one day accept her Divine Son, too.

Evidence to support these views is found in the historical fact that the Moslems occupied Portugal for centuries. At the time when they were finally driven out, the last Moslem chief had a beautiful daughter by the name of Fatima. A Catholic boy fell in love with her, and for him she not only stayed behind when the Moslems left but even embraced the Faith. The young husband was so much in love with her that he changed the name of the town where he lived to Fatima. Thus, the very place where Our Lady appeared in 1917 bears a historical connection to Fatima the daughter of Mohammed.

The final evidence of the relationship of the village of Fatima to the Moslems is the enthusiastic reception that the

Moslems in Africa and India and elsewhere gave to the pilgrim statue of Our Lady of Fatima, as mentioned earlier. Moslems attended the church services in honor of Our Lady; they allowed religious processions and even prayers before their mosques; and in Mozambique the Moslems, who were unconverted, began to be Christian as soon as the statue of Our Lady of Fatima was erected.

Missionaries in the future will, more and more, see that their apostolate among the Moslems will be successful in the measure that they preach Our Lady of Fatima. Mary is the advent of Christ, bringing Christ to the people before Christ Himself is born. In any apologetic endeavor, it is always best to start with that which people already accept. Because the Moslems have a devotion to Mary, our missionaries should be satisfied merely to expand and to develop that devotion, with the full realization that Our Blessed Lady will carry the Moslems the rest of the way to her Divine Son. She is forever a "traitor" in the sense that she will not accept any devotion for herself, but will always bring anyone who is devoted to her to her Divine Son. As those who lose devotion to her lose belief in the Divinity of Christ, so those who intensify devotion to her gradually acquire that belief.

Many of our great missionaries in Africa have already broken down the bitter hatred and prejudices of the Moslems against the Christians through their acts of charity, their schools and hospitals. It now remains to use another approach, namely, that of taking the forty-first chapter of the Koran and showing them that it was taken out of the Gospel of Luke, that Mary could not be, even in their own eyes, the most blessed of all the women of Heaven if she had not also borne One Who was the Savior of the world. If Judith and Esther of the Old Testament were prefigures of Mary, then it may very well be that Fatima herself was a postfigure of Mary! The Moslems should be prepared to acknowledge that, if Fatima must give way in honor to the Blessed Mother, it is because she is different from all the other mothers of the world and that without Christ she would be nothing.

UPDATED BIBLIOGRAPHY

Widely Used English Translations of the Qur'an

Ali, Abdullah Yusuf. *The Holy Qur'an: Text, Translation and Commentary*. 4th ed. Brentwood, Md.: Amana Corp., 1989. Arabic text and translation on opposite pages, extensive notes and commentary.

Arberry, A. J. *The Koran Interpreted*. 1955; London: Allen and Unwin, 1995.

Pickthall, M. M. *The Meaning of the Glorious Koran*. 1930; New York: Meridian, 1997.

Other Translations

Ali, Maulvi Muhammad. *The Holy Qur'an*, Arabic text with English translation and commentary.

Asad, Muhammad. *The Message of the Qur'an*. Gibraltar: Dar al-Andalus, 1984.

Bell, Richard. *The Qur'an: Translated with a Critical Rearrangement of the Surahs*. 2 vols. Edinburgh, 1937–1939. A scholarly work.

Dawood, N. J. *The Koran, A New Translation*. 1955; New York: Penguin, 1980.

Ishaat, Ahmadiyya Anjuman. *Islam*. Lahore, Punjab, India, 1920. With Arabic and English in parallel columns.

Rodwell, J. M. *The Koran*. 1909; London, J. M. Dent; Rutland, Vt.: Charles E. Tuttle, 1994.

Sarwar, Al Haj Hafiz-Ghulam. *Translation of the Holy Qur'an*. From the original Arabic text. Singapore, 1928. In the introduction to his translation the author reviews at length the previous English translations (pp. vii–xlix), namely, those of Sale, Rodwell, Palmer, and Muhammed Ali.

Other Works of Interest

Ahmad, Khurshid. *Islam, Its Meaning and Message.* The Islamic Foundation, 1976.

Andrae, Tor. *Mohammed, the Man and His Faith.* New York, 1936; Dover, 2000.

Bell, Richard. *Introduction to the Qur'an.* Edinburgh, 1953.

———. *The Origin of Islam in Its Christian Environment.* London, 1926.

Blachère, Régis. *Introduction au Coran.* 2d ed. Paris, 1991.

Churches' Committee on Migrant Workers in Europe. *Christians and Muslims Talking Together.* British Council of Churches, 1984.

Cragg, K. *The Call of the Minaret.* 2d ed. Collins, 1986.

———. *Readings in the Qur'an.* London: Collins, 1988.

Daniel, N. *Islam and the West: The Making of an Image.* Oxford: Oneworld, 1997.

Dermenghem, Émile. *Mahomet et la tradition islamique.* Paris, 1930.

Esposito, J. L., ed. *Voices of Resurgent Islam.* Oxford Univ. Press, 1983.

Gaudefroy-Demombynes, Maurice. *Mahomet.* 2d ed. Paris: Albin Michel, 1969.

Gaudeul, J.-M. *Encounter and Clashes: Islam and Christianity in History.* 2 vols. Rome: Pontificio Instituto de Studi Arabi e Islamici, 1984.

Gibb, H. A. R. *Islam: A Historical Survey.* 2d ed. Oxford Univ. Press, 1980.

Hourani, A. *Arabic Thought in the Liberal Age.* 2d ed. Cambridge Univ. Press, 1983.

Irving, T. B. *The Qur'an: Basic Teachings*. The Islamic Foundation, 1979.

Jeffery, A. "The Textual History of the Qur'an". *Journal of the Middle East Society* 2 (1947).

_____. *Materials for the History of the Text of the Qur'an*. Leiden, 1937.

Kennedy, H. *The Prophet and the Age of the Caliphs*. Longmans, 1986.

Lammens, H., S.J. *L'Islam Croyances et Institutions*. Beyrouth, 1926. Translated into several languages, including Arabic.

Levy, R. *The Social Structure of Islam*. 2d ed. London and New York: Routledge, 2000.

Lewis, B., ed. *The World of Islam*. Thames and Hudson, 1976.

Lings, M. *Muhammad: His Life Based on the Earliest Sources*. Allen and Unwin, 1983.

Momen, M. *An Introduction to Shi'i Islam*. Yale Univ. Press, 1985.

Nasr, S. H. *Ideals and Realities of Islam*. Allen and Unwin, 1985.

_____. *Islamic Science: An Illustrated Study*. World of Islam Publishing, 1976.

Nawawi, M. *The Forty Hadith*. Holy Koran Pub. House, 1977.

Nöldeke, Theodor. *Geschichte des Qorans*. Edited by Friedrich Schwally. New York: G. Olms, 1982.

Paret, Rudi. *Mohammed und der Koran*. Stuttgart, 1957.

Parrinder, G. *Jesus in the Qur'an*. Faber, 1965.

Rahman, F. *Islam*. Weidenfeld and Nicolson, 1966.

Schacht, J. *An Introduction to Islamic Law*. Oxford Univ. Press, 1964.

_____, and C. E. Bosworth, eds. *The Legacy of Islam*. Oxford Univ. Press, 1974.

Schuon, F. *Understanding Islam*. 2d ed. Allen and Unwin, 1981.

Sell, Canon. *The Historical Development of the Qur'an.* London, 1927.

Tames, R. *Approaches to Islam.* John Murray, 1982.

Watt, W. M. *Bell's Introduction to the Qur'an.* Edinburgh, 1977.

_____. *Muhammad: Prophet and Statesman.* Oxford Univ. Press, 1977.